DR. KIMBERLEY TAYLOR

Twin Flames: "Solving the Mystery of Love, Challenges, and Transformation."

This book was professionally typeset on Reedsy.
Find out more at reedsy.com

Dedication
To the seekers of truth and love,
To those who dare to journey into the depths of the soul,
May this book guide and inspire you to embrace the challenges,
revelations, and transformations of the twin flame path.
To my own twin flame,
Thank you for the mirror of growth, the fire of transformation,
And the love that transcends lifetimes.
And to all the kindred spirits,
May you find the courage to awaken to your divine purpose and
connect with the infinite within.

"The meeting of two personalities is like the contact of two chemical substances: if there is any reaction, both are transformed."

— Carl Gustav Jung

Contents

Foreword

The inclusion of two authors for the foreword of *Twin Flames: Solving the Mystery of Love, Challenges, and Transformation* was an intentional choice to reflect the core themes of the book—balance, duality, and the transformative power of connection. Rev. Renee and Coach Allen "Ace" Ford offer contrasting yet complementary perspectives, embodying the harmony of masculine and feminine energies, as well as the diversity of experiences that shape the twin flame journey.

Rev. Renee's heartfelt account speaks to the miraculous, life-saving impact of Dr. Kimberley Taylor's healing gifts and the profound soul connection that transcends time and space. In contrast, Coach Ace's story illustrates the unexpected, transformative nature of platonic soul partnerships, showcasing how twin flame energy can manifest beyond romantic relationships. Together, their voices create a dynamic balance that highlights the universal truth at the heart of this book: love, in its many forms, is the most powerful force of all—one that defies logic, transcends boundaries, and fosters growth, healing, and spiritual awakening.

You are in for a treat Dear Reader! Because Dr. Kimberley Taylor, the author of this amazing book, has continuously devoted most of her adult life to unconditionally helping others grow and heal within. I was blessed to meet Kimberley over a decade ago, while we were attending a spiritual event, and felt an instant soul kinship toward her. We had much in common, complimentary spiritual interests and quickly became good friends. But the soulfully solidifying miracle between us was yet to come.

Let's fast forward to an incredible sacred journey to the ancient Peruvian Mountains. During an "other worldly" day at Machu Picchu, 82 members of the group were allowed to pass through the level ground / short trail back to the historic site entrance and restaurant. Suddenly, a man literally appeared out of nowhere, placing a small rope across the trail path, sternly telling my brother, Kimberley and I, "no" you are not allowed to pass. No matter our pleas, this "person" refused to allow passage, and we were forced to walk a labor-intensive path down and back up the mountain. During this trek, my arm became numb, with excruciating pain in my chest. Yes, I was having yet another heart attack. You see Dear Readers, this was the fourth Near Death Experience (NDE) I had over recent years, due to a severe chronic health condition. Me being alive baffles doctors and has left them pondering, why is she still here? Well, the truth is, during each of these NDE's the veil "thinned" a bit more, and I became closer and closer to God, the Archangels and Divine. During one of my more serious and transformational NDE's the Archangels – Archangel Gabriel to be specific, assured me that he would still breathe for me while I was on Earth. Because of my role in the sacred Peruvian journey group, I tried to remain stoic, while enduring extreme pain, without collapsing. Once back at the restaurant, Kimberley said, "the Angels are only letting me feel 20% of your pain and I can barely stand it. I cannot even believe you are sitting upright. Do you want me to try to help you? Emergency personnel could never make it to Machu Picchu in time." I said YES! Please, I will be forever grateful for any assistance. It was a miracle! For the next 20 minutes Dr. Kimberley poured Angelic Reiki healing energy into me, and it worked! While Dr. Kimberley was connected to the Archangels, the severe pain subsided, and I was able to function again. Dr. Kimberley saved my life that day, and I am forever grateful.

Our Soul Kin bond strengthened tremendously that day, on many energetic levels. I trust Dr. Kimberley with my life forever more! And you can too! In addition to Dr. Kimberley's the healing gifts and spiritual talents, shared with family, friends, clients and anyone open to healing and growing, God / the Divine Universe have placed a multitude of Twin Flame scenarios in her path over the past decades. You will be delighted to find this Twin Flame book is ALL true, based on real experiences, Divine guidance, outcomes, practical spirituality and much more! You will find this book has been designed to inspire the reader to look deep within and find YOUR Truth! It is filled with thought-provoking tools to help you uncover hidden feelings and emotions, meaningful guidance and heart opening Twin Flame stories, and this is an amazing opportunity to bring much more love into YOUR life. Afterward, I do encourage you Dear Reader, to retain your forward momentum by keeping a close connection with Dr. Kimberley's Twin Flame works and healing offerings. As she will be offering amazing new spiritually guided classes, healing retreats, sacred journeys and divinely connected community opportunities.

Peace and Love begins within, Rev. Renee

When I first received the call from my dear friend, Dr. Kimberley Taylor, and she told me she was writing a book, the joy I felt was immeasurable. I met Dr. Kimberley Taylor nearly a decade before that call, during a pivotal time in my life. I was an aspiring life coach, navigating a profound shift in my spiritual beliefs, standing at the threshold of a deeper connection to divinity and purpose. Guided by my own spiritual mentor, I found myself working at a metaphysical shop—an unexpected step that would soon introduce me to the concept of a "Twin Flame."

Transitioning from the classroom of spiritual theory to the practical space of real-life application was nerve-wracking. I knew I was gifted, capable of speaking the language of the soul—one that inspires, uplifts, and guides others toward transformation. But at the time, I didn't realize that this wasn't just about starting a new job; it was the beginning of a life-altering journey. On my very first day, I met Dr. Kimberley Taylor—"Kim" to me, or as I affectionately call her, my "Wister," a blend of *wife* and *sister.* Yes, I know how that sounds—let me explain.

I was sitting in the employee lounge, sipping tea, quietly observing the diverse group around me—people from all walks of life, each with fascinating stories of how they'd arrived there. I felt small, overwhelmed, and uncertain about my place among them. Then, I heard the faint click of a door opening, followed by a gentle, "I'll see you again soon." Moments later, she appeared—confident, poised, and unapologetically herself. I instinctively tried to avoid her gaze, but that's not how Kimberley operates. She walked right up to me and introduced herself with a simple, "Hi, I'm Kimberley." Trying to be charming, I replied, "Hi, Kim. I'm Allen, but everyone calls me Ace!"

With a slight arch of her brow and a firm, matter-of-fact tone, she corrected me, "It's Kimberley." I grinned mischievously and teased, "Okay then... *Kim-ber-ley.*"

In that moment, I decided I didn't like her. Who corrects someone on a nickname—a universal sign of endearment, right? But that brief clash of personalities sparked something neither of us could explain. Over time, I'd whisper "Kim" under my breath whenever I saw her, and she'd meet my playful defiance with a knowing smile.

As we got to know each other, we discovered an unexpected connection. On paper, we couldn't have been more different. I'm a vibrant, expressive, unapologetically queer Black man, twenty years her junior, navigating life with flair and a healthy dose of rebellion. She's a grounded, well-educated, world-traveled white woman, conservative in demeanor, married with children my age and older. We are, in every sense, the embodiment of an "odd couple." Yet, through our friendship, I learned that the soul knows no gender, no race, no labels. Love transcends all of that.

Kimberley became more than just a friend; she became my mirror, my catalyst, my *Wister*. Our bond taught me that real love—whether platonic, romantic, or spiritual—is expansive. It breaks down walls, shatters illusions, and accelerates growth. Where I brought boldness and color, she brought wisdom and grounding. Together, we navigated life's lessons, shared dreams, and supported each other through both triumphs and trials.

Through Kimberley, I discovered my own version of a Twin Flame connection. Not one defined by romance, but by the sacred reflection of two souls who challenge and uplift each other in ways that defy logic. Over the years, I've grown from merely surviving to thriving—transforming into a successful coach and businessman, living out dreams I once thought were out of reach.

I wholeheartedly recommend *Twin Flame: A Journey of Love, Challenge, and Transformation* by Dr. Kimberley Taylor. This book is more than words on a page—it's an invitation to explore the depths of connection, the beauty of soul growth, and the transformative power of love in all its forms. Open your heart and allow this journey to awaken something sacred within you.

As the songwriters Bert Kaempfert and Milt Gabler so beautifully wrote:

"L is for the way you look at me
O is for the only one I see
V is very, very extraordinary
E is even more than anyone that you adore can love..."

To my dear Wister, thank you for the gift of your friendship and for the courage to share your story with the world. To every reader, I declare abundance, inspiration, and transformation over your life. May you find within these pages not just words, but reflections of your own soul's journey.

With love and gratitude,

Coach Allen "Ace" Ford

Life Coach & Strategist Extraordinaire

Preface

The twin flame journey is one of the most profound and enigmatic paths a soul can undertake. It is a journey filled with joy and despair, connection and separation, awakening and growth. It transcends traditional notions of love, compelling those who embark upon it to confront their deepest fears, discover their greatest strengths, and embrace the full spectrum of their humanity.

This book was born from my own exploration of the twin flame phenomenon—a topic that, over the years, has fascinated, mystified, and profoundly transformed me. Along the way, I have encountered countless individuals whose lives were forever changed by these rare and intense connections. Their stories, lessons, and revelations have served as both a guide and a mirror, helping me piece together the intricate puzzle of what it means to love at the soul level.

In these pages, you will find insights gathered from years of observation, study, and personal reflection. My aim is to unravel the mysteries surrounding twin flames and offer a balanced perspective—one that honors both the beauty and the challenges of this journey. This book is not a definitive answer to what twin flames are; rather, it is an invitation to explore the possibilities, reflect on your experiences, and discover your own truths.

Whether you are new to the concept of twin flames, currently navigating a twin flame connection, or simply curious about the trans formative nature of soul relationships, my hope is that this book will resonate with you. It is a compass for those seeking clarity, a balm for those in the midst of struggle, and a celebration of the love that unites us all.

May this book inspire you to embrace your journey, trust the process, and open your heart to the limitless power of love.

With gratitude,

Dr. Kimberley Taylor

Acknowledgments

This book would not have been possible without the love, guidance, and support of those who have inspired me on my journey. To my mentors, friends, and family who believed in the power of transformation and healing, I am forever grateful. Special thanks to those who shared their Twin Flame experiences, offering courage and wisdom that now flow through these pages.

Prologue

There is a connection so profound, so all-encompassing, that it transcends the boundaries of time, space, and understanding. It is a love that is not merely found but rediscovered—a spark of recognition that ignites the depths of the soul. This is the essence of the twin flame journey.

In every corner of the world, people have felt this inexplicable pull—a bond that defies logic and awakens something ancient within. For some, it manifests as a chance encounter that shifts their entire existence. For others, it emerges as a lingering presence, a sense that someone, somewhere, is meant to walk beside them on this earthly plane. Yet, for all who experience it, the journey of twin flames is one of transformation, challenge, and the ultimate search for truth.

This journey is not for the faint of heart. It will demand everything you are and everything you are yet to become. It will reveal the shadows you hide from, the fears you bury, and the light you were always destined to embrace. Twin flames are not merely partners—they are mirrors, reflecting back the parts of ourselves that we most need to see. Through their gaze, we are forced to confront our wounds, heal our pasts, and step into our higher purpose.

And yet, as daunting as this path may seem, it is also one of the greatest gifts life can offer. For within the intensity lies a love that is unconditional, a connection that is sacred, and a purpose that is divine. The twin flame journey is not just about finding another—it is about finding yourself.

As you open this book, know that you are not alone. Whether you are just beginning to sense the call of your twin flame or are deep in the throes of its trials, this journey belongs to you. It is as unique as your soul, yet it is part of something greater—a universal dance of love, growth, and connection.

Let these pages serve as a guide, a companion, and a source of understanding. Together, we will explore the mysteries of twin flames, unravel the lessons they bring, and embrace the beauty of transformation. For this is not just a story about love; it is a story about becoming whole.

Welcome to the journey.

Introduction

If you are reading this book, you have likely encountered the concept of Twin Flames or found yourself intrigued by the idea at some point. Twin Flames have become a captivating yet controversial topic, raising many questions about love, connection, and spiritual purpose. There is no shortage of perspectives on what a Twin Flame is—or isn't. The purpose of this book is to offer clarity, share new insights, and perhaps reveal a more complete truth about this profound subject.

For over a decade, I have had the unique opportunity to witness and study various relationships that have been classified as Twin Flame connections. These relationships spanned all kinds—platonic, familial, romantic, professional—and each carried its own powerful energy. What initially began as an interest in a handful of relationships evolved into a deeper fascination with the impact these connections have had on people across time, geography, and even belief systems.

The more I observed, the more I noticed a pattern: many Twin Flame connections, despite being touted as the pinnacle of spiritual partnership, were often accompanied by significant challenges. I found myself asking, *"If Twin Flames are meant to embody the highest and most loving relationship possible, why is there so much agony, struggle, and strife in those that I have witnessed?"* Could we have misunderstood the purpose, or even the definition, of Twin Flames? This question set me on a path to uncover a greater understanding of these connections.

This book is the culmination of years of observation, study, and contemplation. It is a deep dive into the heart of Twin Flame dynamics, and through this journey, I hope to share with you the insights, lessons, and perhaps the treasure I found hidden within. Whether you are on your own Twin Flame journey, know someone who is, or simply seek greater clarity on the topic, this book is here to offer a fresh perspective. Let us explore together what it means to be truly connected, to love deeply, and to discover the divine purpose in our most intense relationships.

1

Definition and Origin of Twin Flame

Let's begin by defining Twin and Flame separately.

"Twin." *Merriam-Webster.com Dictionary*, Merriam-Webster, https://www.merriam-webster.com/dictionary/twin. Accessed 15 Mar. 2022.

Noun

1a: either of two offspring produced in the same pregnancy

b: Twins *plural*: GEMINI

2: one of two person or things closely related to or resembling each other

3: a compound crystal composed of two adjoining crystals or parts of crystals of the same kind that share a common plane of atoms

Adjective

1: born with one other or as a pair at one birth

2a: made up of two similar, related or connected members or parts :DOUBLE

b: paired in a close or necessary relationship: MATCHING

c: having or consisting of two identical units

d: being one of a pair

5

Verb

transitive verb

1: to bring together in close association : COUPLE

2: DUPLICATE, MATCH

intransitive verb

1: to bring forth twins

2: of a crystal: to grow in a compound form with two adjoining sections that share a common plane of atoms

"Flame." *Merriam-Webster.com Dictionary*, Merriam-Webster, https://www.merriam-webster.com/dictionary/flame. Accessed 15 Mar. 2022

Noun

1: the glowing gaseous part of a fire

2a: a state of blazing combustion

b: a condition or appearance suggesting a flame or burning; such as

(1) Burning zeal or passion

(2) A strong reddish-orange color

3: BRILLIANCE, BRIGHTNESS

4: SWEETHEART_SENSE

5: the memory, reputation, or beliefs of a deceased person *broadly*: MEMORY (keeper of the *flame*)

6: an angry, hostile or abusive electronic message

Verb

intransitive verb

1: to burn with a flame: BLAZE

2a: to burst or break out violently or passionately (*flaming with indignation*)

b: to send an angry, hostile, or abusive electronic message

3: to shine brightly: GLOW (color *flaming* up in her cheeks)

transitive verb

1: to send or convey by means of flame (*flame* a message by signal fires)

2: to treat or affect with flame: such as

a: to sear, sterilize, or destroy by fire

b: **FLAMBÉ**

3: to send an angry, hostile, or abusive electronic message to or about

The Origins of the Twin Flame Concept

To understand the Twin Flame phenomenon, it's essential to examine the roots of the idea itself. While modern interpretations of Twin Flames often blend mysticism and spirituality, the term and its implications draw from a mix of ancient philosophy, religious texts, and more recent spiritual teachings. Here, we delve into these origins and explore how the concept of Twin Flames evolved.

One of the earliest philosophical mentions of a similar concept appears in the works of the ancient Greek philosopher Plato. In his *Symposium* (circa 385 BCE), Plato introduces a myth told by the playwright Aristophanes, in which humans were once powerful, androgynous beings with four arms, four legs, and two faces. These beings were considered a threat by the gods, so Zeus split them in half, condemning them to a life of wandering in search of their other half to feel complete again. Plato's narrative of human beings longing for their "missing half" is one of the earliest documented accounts resembling what we now call Twin Flames. The story suggests that our deepest connections might come from this primordial longing to reunite with a partner who shares our essence.

7

While Plato's allegory provides a foundation for the Twin Flame concept, the actual term "Twin Flame" wasn't widely used until much later. In the modern era, the idea was popularized by Elizabeth Clare Prophet, a prominent yet controversial spiritual leader in the New Age movement. In her 1999 book, *Soul Mates and Twin Flames: The Spiritual Dimension of Love and Relationships*, Prophet introduced the term "Twin Flames" to a wider audience. Her teachings focused on spiritual connections that transcend earthly love, suggesting that each soul has a counterpart with whom it shares a unique and eternal bond. This relationship, according to Prophet, serves a higher purpose, promoting individual spiritual growth and cosmic harmony.

The concept of Twin Flames gained additional traction with the rise of online spiritual communities, notably Twin Flames Universe, led by Jeff and Shaleia Ayan. The Ayans' approach includes the belief that Twin Flames are created as two parts of one soul, split at the moment of creation, destined to reunite. Paula Hardy, whose twin sister Stephanie Zimmerman is an active member of the Twin Flames Universe, explains that "God created two parts of us to have basically one soul." Hardy elaborates that these two parts are mirror images of each other and are brought together by divine forces to heal and elevate each other. This concept has reached a broad audience through social media and popular platforms, including the Netflix documentary series *Escaping Twin Flames*, furthering the belief that Twin Flames are "two halves of the same soul" intended to find completion through union.

Religious texts also hold interpretations that seem to echo the idea of Twin Flames. Some theorists propose that the story of Adam and Eve in the Bible reflects this connection. According to the story in Genesis, God created Eve from Adam's rib, making them "bone of bone and flesh of flesh." From a symbolic perspective, this pairing represents an intimate and divinely orchestrated bond, one that suggests a union meant for partnership and harmony. In some interpretations, Adam and Eve are seen as "twins" in essence, created as complements to each other. This view aligns with the "twin" aspect of the Twin Flame concept, though it does not fully account for the idea of a "flame," or a journey of separation and reunification.

The concept of the "flame" in Twin Flames speaks to a more mystical and energetic dimension. Many proponents of the Twin Flame theory suggest that each soul is split before birth and that these two halves are destined to reunite after a journey of individual growth and healing. In this journey, the "flame" symbolizes a trans formative spiritual force that propels each soul toward wholeness and enlightenment. However, this idealized journey brings its own challenges: as human beings, we are rarely free from the influences of ego, insecurity, and other emotional barriers. These human limitations cast doubt on the notion of achieving "completeness," as healing in the human experience is often ongoing and imperfect.

To date, there is no scientific evidence to substantiate the Twin Flame concept, and it remains a theory within spiritual and theosophical circles. Skeptics argue that Twin Flame relationships are merely projections of our desires for fulfillment and intimacy. Some researchers point out that elements of Twin Flame narratives—such as the idea of a partner who reflects one's inner self and forces personal growth—could be explained through psychological concepts like projection, attachment theory, or even trauma bonding. Nevertheless, for those who believe in Twin Flames, the lack of scientific validation does not detract from their experiences.

Theories around Twin Flames continue to evolve, shaped by spiritual communities and the individual stories of those who feel they've encountered their counterpart. Whether seen as an allegory for self-discovery or a divine truth, the notion of Twin Flames challenges our understanding of love, intimacy, and personal growth. This book seeks to explore these complexities and provide a balanced perspective on the often enigmatic and deeply personal journey that Twin Flames represent.

Key Takeaways

- Reflect on how ancient philosophies and spiritual teachings shape the concept of Twin Flames.
- Which part of the historical perspective resonated most with you?

Personal Reflections

1. Have you ever felt the kind of connection described in Plato's allegory of two halves longing to reunite? If so, how has it shaped your relationships?
2. How do you feel about the idea that Twin Flames are not necessarily romantic but may serve as mirrors for growth?

Exercises

- Research and write about another cultural or spiritual interpretation of soul connections. How does it compare to the Twin Flame concept?
- Meditate on the idea of "divine wholeness." Journal how it might feel to embody wholeness rather than longing for

completion.

Closing Thought
"Every soul's journey begins with understanding its roots."

2

Ideology of a Twin Flame Relationship

In understanding the ideology of a Twin Flame relationship, it's important to consider the qualities and dynamics that define it. A Twin Flame relationship is thought to be one of the most intense, trans formative, and sometimes tumultuous relationships a person can experience. Those who believe in Twin Flames describe an unmistakable sense of recognition—a pull that seems to stem from the soul itself, as if meeting this person awakens a deeply rooted familiarity, a feeling that one has known the other across lifetimes.

One of the most intriguing characteristics of Twin Flames is this magnetic connection that seems unbreakable, almost like an energetic tether binding the two. They may discover remarkable similarities in their life experiences, values, and interests, even if their paths have been wildly different. Often, Twin Flames share similar emotional wounds, whether from neglect, abandonment, or other hardships, which adds another layer of shared understanding. These complementary qualities can also foster a deep connection and create a potent environment for personal healing and growth.

Yet, this intense connection isn't without its challenges. In many cases, a Twin Flame serves as a mirror, reflecting both the beautiful and the unresolved parts of one's soul. For all the love and comfort a Twin Flame brings, they can also reflect back fears, insecurities, unprocessed trauma, and doubts that the other may not yet be ready to confront. While one might expect a Twin Flame to help their counterpart work through these issues, the reality is often much more complex. The relationship frequently stirs up unhealed wounds, bringing them to the surface and creating a level of discomfort that can be difficult for both parties to manage.

Many sources and spiritual teachers suggest that Twin Flame relationships unfold in stages, though scientific studies to support or refute these claims do not exist. These stages reflect a progression that resembles a journey of growth, but they can also lead to repeated cycles of tension and separation. Here are the generally accepted stages of a Twin Flame relationship:

1. Yearning Stage

The journey often begins with a sensation of yearning, where one feels an unexplained emptiness or sense that something significant is missing. Some people report having dreams, premonitions, or recurring signs that foreshadow the arrival of their Twin Flame. This stage can create a strong desire to connect with someone who seems almost mythical, yet feels essential to the soul.

2. Meeting Stage

When Twin Flames first meet, the connection can be immediate and electrifying. People often describe an intense recognition and an unshakable pull toward this person. This meeting feels extraordinary, as if encountering someone who embodies a piece of oneself that has been missing. Even if they are strangers, there is an inexplicable familiarity, a feeling that they've known each other for lifetimes.

3. Falling in Love

The initial attraction deepens, often resulting in a euphoric and exhilarating connection. For those in romantic Twin Flame relationships, this can mean falling in love quickly and intensely, as if all previous experiences of love were only leading up to this. In non-romantic Twin Flame connections, this stage still brings about a powerful bond, devoid of physical desire but marked by a desire to know each other's soul deeply.

4. Honeymoon Period

As the connection deepens, the Twin Flames experience a period of bliss, intimacy, and spiritual bonding. This stage is marked by harmony and a feeling of completion, where both partners feel at ease and deeply connected. They may discover spiritual synchronicities, shared dreams, or heightened intuition regarding each other's needs and thoughts.

5. Turmoil or Testing Period

The honeymoon phase eventually gives way to tension as the differences between the two emerge. Old wounds and insecurities resurface, and these can challenge the idealized version of the relationship that both have held. For many, this period becomes a trial of faith and resilience, as past traumas and vulnerabilities rise to the surface, challenging each partner to confront unresolved issues within themselves.

6. Runner and Chaser

In response to the intensity of these trials, one partner (often the less emotionally prepared) may attempt to flee from the relationship. This is known as the "runner" phase, while the other partner, typically the more mature or secure, takes on the role of the "chaser." The chaser often tries to repair the relationship, feeling responsible for keeping it intact and attempting to work through issues. This runner-chaser dynamic can persist for years and may cycle back and forth multiple times, each episode intensifying the emotional bond and testing the limits of patience and endurance.

7. Surrender and Dissolution

Over time, the relationship reaches a point where the individuals become more comfortable with their own insecurities and vulnerabilities. If both Twin Flames are willing to surrender their defenses and address their wounds, the relationship may transition to a more stable and grounded connection. However, if one or both partners cannot come to terms with these aspects of themselves, the relationship may dissolve, either temporarily or permanently. This stage can bring tremendous personal growth, as each individual learns the value of acceptance and the importance of inner peace, whether or not they are able to maintain the relationship.

8. Oneness

For Twin Flames who reach this stage, the bond becomes stronger, often transcending the ups and downs they've experienced. The individuals find a sense of oneness with each other and within themselves, creating a relationship based on mutual respect, understanding, and support. However, not all Twin Flame relationships reach this stage, as it requires both parties to achieve a level of self-awareness and spiritual maturity that allows them to see past ego and insecurities. In many cases, the dissolution stage becomes the endpoint if one or both partners are unable to fully integrate their experiences and achieve harmony within themselves.

The Twin Flame relationship ideology is both compelling and complex. It presents an ideal of ultimate love and union while

also requiring individuals to confront some of the deepest and
most difficult aspects of themselves. Twin Flames are said to
reflect back to each other what they need to heal, and while this
can lead to profound personal growth, it can also create cycles
of pain and separation.

While scientific research does not confirm the existence of
Twin Flames, the concept remains powerful for many, offering a
spiritual framework for understanding some of the most intense
relationships we encounter. Twin Flame relationships continue
to captivate people worldwide, presenting a paradoxical vision
of love that demands both surrender and strength, intimacy and
independence, connection and self-discovery.

Key Takeaways

- Explore the concept of recognition, mirroring, and spiritual
  growth within a Twin Flame relationship.
- Reflect on the described stages of Twin Flame relationships.

Personal Reflections

1. Which stage of the Twin Flame journey do you resonate
   with most? Why?
2. What personal experiences have mirrored the challenges
   and growth described in Twin Flame dynamics?

Exercises

- Create a timeline of a significant relationship in your life.
  Identify any moments that align with the stages of the Twin
  Flame journey.

· Write about a time when you felt mirrored by someone else. How did it impact your self-awareness?

Closing Thought

"Every stage of the journey, whether joyful or painful, is a step toward deeper understanding."

3

An Introduction to Twin Flames

The concept of Twin Flames has captured imaginations world-wide, often inspiring visions of fated romance and soul-deep connection. Unlike conventional relationships, Twin Flames transcend physical attraction, friendship, and even traditional love as we commonly understand it. These connections are often described as two halves of the same soul, reunited through a cosmic plan to achieve growth, healing, and spiritual evolution. Yet, this journey is far from easy or predictable. For many, encountering their Twin Flame is both a blessing and a profound challenge.

This chapter explores what defines a Twin Flame connection, what sets it apart from other relationships, and why these bonds are often as trans formative as they are complex.

What Are Twin Flames?

Twin Flames are believed to be two souls sharing the same essence or energy, sometimes described as "split" halves of a singular soul. Upon reincarnation, these two halves find each other in human form, experiencing a bond that is unparalleled in intensity, love, and understanding. This connection often evokes a profound sense of familiarity and recognition, as though encountering a part of oneself in another.

The Twin Flame journey, however, is as challenging as it is inspiring. While the two souls are deeply drawn to one another, their connection often compels them to confront unresolved aspects of their inner lives. This process is not only trans formative but also deeply introspective, as each partner is invited to embrace both their strengths and shadows.

Characteristics of a Twin Flame Connection

While every Twin Flame journey is unique, certain characteristics commonly define these connections:

1. Instant Recognition: Meeting a Twin Flame often evokes an immediate and profound sense of familiarity, as if encountering someone known across lifetimes.
2. Intense Emotional Bond: Twin Flames frequently experience heightened emotions in each other's presence. These feelings can range from euphoric joy to overwhelming vulnerability.
3. Spiritual Awakening: The encounter often acts as a catalyst for profound spiritual growth, offering new insights into the self and the universe.
4. Mirroring Effect: Twin Flames reflect both the light and shadow aspects of one another, creating opportunities for deep healing and self-awareness.

5. Push-and-Pull Dynamics: Known as the "Runner-Chaser" phase, this dynamic reflects the fear and longing each partner may feel, often leading to cycles of closeness and separation.

How Twin Flames Differ from Soulmates

Though often confused, Twin Flames and Soulmates represent distinct spiritual concepts. Soulmates are individuals from one's soul family—those with whom one shares a strong bond. These connections may appear in various forms, including romantic partners, friends, or mentors, and their purpose is typically to offer love, support, and companionship.

Twin Flames, in contrast, represent a singular and unique connection. Unlike the harmony often associated with Soulmate relationships, Twin Flame bonds are characterized by their intensity and transformational nature. The purpose of a Twin Flame connection is not merely companionship but mutual evolution, healing, and awakening to one's highest potential.

The Purpose of Twin Flame Relationships

The Twin Flame journey transcends traditional notions of romance, emphasizing profound personal and spiritual growth. Through their connection, Twin Flames are compelled to face deep-seated fears, heal past traumas, and evolve as individuals. Though this process can be both exhilarating and painful, it ultimately fosters a sense of wholeness and alignment with one's authentic self.

In some spiritual traditions, Twin Flames are believed to share a higher mission or purpose on Earth. Together, they may work to uplift those around them, contributing to the collective good. This shared purpose infuses the Twin Flame journey with meaning and direction, transforming it into a path of service as well as personal fulfillment.

The Stages of the Twin Flame Journey

The Twin Flame experience often unfolds in distinct stages, each offering unique challenges and lessons:

1. Yearning and Searching: Before meeting their Twin Flame, individuals may feel a profound sense of longing, as though something essential is missing. This stage often involves spiritual growth and self-discovery, preparing the individual for the connection ahead.
2. Recognition and Union: Upon meeting, Twin Flames experience an intense sense of recognition, often described as "coming home." This stage is marked by feelings of unconditional love and deep familiarity.
3. Crisis and Mirroring: As the connection deepens, Twin Flames reflect unresolved wounds and insecurities, leading to emotional challenges and opportunities for growth.
4. Runner and Chaser Dynamic: One partner may pull away (the Runner) due to the intensity of the connection, while the other seeks to bridge the gap (the Chaser). This phase emphasizes the need for individual healing and self-reliance.
5. Surrender and Self-Realization: Both partners reach a state of acceptance, focusing on their own healing and

spiritual growth. This stage is characterized by inner peace and clarity.

6. Reunion and Co-Creation: If both individuals have evolved sufficiently, they may reunite in a harmonious partnership, channeling their connection into a shared mission or purpose.

Key Takeaways

- Reflect on the differences between Twin Flames and Soul-mates.
- Consider the purpose of Twin Flame relationships in fostering growth and awakening.

Personal Reflections

1. How do you feel about the idea that Twin Flames are not necessarily harmonious, but transformative?
2. Have you ever experienced a connection that felt like it had a higher purpose?

Exercises

- Write a letter to yourself reflecting on how relationships in your life have challenged and shaped you.
- Imagine what "reunion with the self" might look like. Sketch or describe this vision.

Closing Thought

"Transformation begins with recognizing the sacred in every connection."

4

Types of Twin Flame Relationships

Twin Flame relationships manifest in various forms, each offering unique dynamics, challenges, and lessons. While every Twin Flame connection is distinct, these relationships generally serve as powerful catalysts for personal and spiritual growth. By understanding the different types of Twin Flame bonds, we can better appreciate the diversity of experiences and the trans formative potential they hold.

This chapter explores the key types of Twin Flame relationships, their defining characteristics, and their spiritual purposes.

1. The Mirror Twin Flame Relationship

The Mirror Twin Flame connection is perhaps the most well-known and trans formative type. In this dynamic, each partner acts as a mirror, reflecting the other's hidden fears, unresolved traumas, and shadow aspects.

Key Characteristics:

- Intense Reflection: Partners reflect both strengths and vulnerabilities, encouraging self-awareness.
- Emotional Triggers: Interactions often evoke strong emotions, revealing insecurities and unresolved issues.
- Personal Growth: The mirroring effect accelerates inner healing, self-acceptance, and emotional resilience.

Purpose:

The Mirror Twin Flame relationship serves to uncover and heal deep-seated wounds. By embracing these reflections, individuals gain clarity about their authentic selves and can ultimately achieve unconditional love and self-acceptance.

2. The Healing Twin Flame Relationship

The Healing Twin Flame connection focuses on emotional and spiritual healing. This type of relationship often forms when one or both partners are recovering from past trauma or hardship. Twin Flames in this dynamic act as compassionate healers, providing support and safety.

Key Characteristics:

- Mutual Support: Partners prioritize helping each other heal and grow.
- Emotional Intimacy: Vulnerability and transparency are core to the relationship.
- Compassionate Understanding: Both individuals cultivate patience and empathy.

24

Purpose:

The Healing Twin Flame relationship creates a safe space for recovery and rejuvenation. Through this connection, both partners rebuild inner strength, trust, and the ability to embrace love fully.

3. The Teacher Twin Flame Relationship

In the Teacher Twin Flame connection, one or both partners serve as guides, helping the other achieve spiritual awakening or personal growth. These relationships often leave a lasting impact, even if they are short-lived.

Key Characteristics:

- Mentorship: One partner often provides wisdom, guidance, or perspective.
- Awakening Experiences: Encounters often lead to life-changing realizations.
- Temporary Connection: These relationships may not last long but are deeply trans formative.

Purpose:

The Teacher Twin Flame relationship exists to inspire new understanding and spiritual growth. It challenges individuals to explore their potential and align with their life purpose.

4. The Creative Twin Flame Relationship

The Creative Twin Flame connection centers on shared creative

25

or artistic expression. Partners in this type of relationship inspire each other to pursue their creative passions, often collaborating on meaningful projects.

Key Characteristics:

- Collaborative Efforts: Partners feel compelled to create together, whether in art, music, or business.
- Mutual Inspiration: Each partner encourages the other's creativity and self-expression.
- Shared Mission: Their work often aims to uplift or inspire others.

Purpose:

The Creative Twin Flame relationship channels the bond into creative endeavors, producing beauty, insight, or innovation that benefits the world. It highlights the trans formative power of shared inspiration.

5. The Catalyst Twin Flame Relationship

Catalyst Twin Flame relationships are brief but intense, sparking rapid transformation in both partners. These connections often reveal fears, insecurities, or patterns that need to change, propelling individuals toward growth.

Key Characteristics:

- Short but Powerful: These relationships may be brief but leave a lasting impact.

- Intense Transformation: The connection demands deep personal change and self-reflection.
- Challenging Yet Rewarding: Although difficult, the lessons learned are invaluable.

Purpose:

The Catalyst Twin Flame relationship exists to trigger profound growth and change. By facing their deepest fears, both partners clear the way for a new phase of life and a stronger sense of self.

6. The Harmonious Twin Flame Relationship

Harmonious Twin Flames have achieved a high level of self-awareness and spiritual maturity. This type of relationship is marked by balance, mutual respect, and unconditional love.

Key Characteristics:

- Balanced Energy: Both partners embody inner harmony and stability.
- Peaceful Connection: The relationship is characterized by calmness, joy, and mutual understanding.
- Aligned Purpose: Partners often share a mission or goal that contributes positively to others.

Purpose:

The Harmonious Twin Flame relationship demonstrates the beauty of unconditional love and balance. This connection

27

allows both partners to grow spiritually while inspiring and uplifting those around them.

7. The Union of Purpose Twin Flame Relationship

In this type of Twin Flame relationship, the connection is centered on a shared mission or calling. These relationships emphasize service and contribution over personal fulfillment.

Key Characteristics:

- Shared Calling: Both partners feel a deep sense of purpose tied to their connection.
- High-Level Dedication: The relationship requires commitment to a greater cause.
- Lasting Legacy: Their work leaves a meaningful impact beyond the relationship itself.

Purpose:
The Union of Purpose Twin Flame relationship highlights the power of love in action. Through their connection, partners contribute to the well-being of others and fulfill a divine mission.

Navigating Different Types of Twin Flame Relationships

Understanding the type of Twin Flame relationship you are experiencing can provide valuable insights and guidance. Each connection offers unique challenges and rewards, encouraging growth, healing, and transformation.

No matter the type, Twin Flame relationships push us to embrace love in its purest form. By honoring the lessons within each connection, we deepen our understanding of ourselves and our purpose in the world.

Embracing the Purpose of Your Twin Flame Connection

Whether your Twin Flame relationship serves as a mirror, a healer, or a source of creative inspiration, its ultimate purpose is to guide you toward self-discovery, love, and growth. Each connection is sacred in its own right, offering valuable lessons that bring us closer to our highest selves.

As we journey through the complexities of these relationships, we uncover the trans formative power of love and the wisdom it reveals within us.

Key Takeaways

- Reflect on the various types of Twin Flame connections (Mirror, Healing, Catalyst, etc.).
- Which type of relationship do you feel you've experienced, if any?

Personal Reflections

1. Which type of Twin Flame relationship resonates most with your journey?
2. How have different connections in your life taught you unique lessons?

Exercises

- Journal about a connection in your life that you feel was transformative. Which type of Twin Flame relationship does it align with?
- Reflect on the purpose of your current relationships. Write about the lessons they are teaching you.

Closing Thought

"Every relationship is a teacher, guiding us toward greater understanding."

Navigating Twin Flame Dynamics – Practical Tools and Insights

Navigating a Twin Flame relationship is a journey of profound growth, requiring emotional resilience, self-awareness, and spiritual alignment. Unlike conventional relationships, Twin Flame connections defy ordinary expectations and demand deeper levels of reflection and healing. The intensity of this journey often uncovers hidden aspects of the self, presenting both challenges and opportunities for transformation.

This chapter offers practical strategies to navigate the complexities of Twin Flame dynamics, focusing on self-healing, emotional balance, and spiritual growth.

1. Practicing Self-Awareness and Reflection

Twin Flames act as mirrors, revealing the hidden aspects of one another's psyche. Cultivating self-awareness is essential to navigating these intense reflections with clarity and grace.

Steps to Cultivate Self-Awareness:

- Journaling: Regularly write about your thoughts, emotions, and reactions, particularly after interactions with your Twin Flame. Reflect on patterns or triggers that surface.
- Mindfulness Meditation: Observe your thoughts and emotions without judgment. This practice fosters presence and allows you to process feelings constructively.
- Introspective Questions: Ask reflective questions like, "What am I learning about myself in this moment?" or "What belief might be fueling this reaction?"

By embracing self-awareness, you can approach challenges as opportunities for growth rather than sources of conflict.

2. Balancing Emotions and Reactions

The emotional intensity of a Twin Flame relationship can be overwhelming. Learning to manage and balance emotions is vital for maintaining stability and fostering healthy communication.

Techniques for Emotional Balance:

- Breath work: Use techniques like the 4-7-8 method (inhale for 4 seconds, hold for 7, exhale for 8) to calm your nervous system.
- Emotional Freedom Techniques (EFT): Tap specific points on the body to release stress and regulate emotions.
- Grounding Practices: Engage in activities like walking bare-

foot on grass or holding grounding crystals (e.g., hematite, black tourmaline) to reconnect with stability.

Balanced emotions enable clear communication and thoughtful decision-making, even in moments of conflict.

3. Establishing Healthy Boundaries

The intensity of a Twin Flame connection can blur personal boundaries, leading to emotional overwhelm or codependency. Setting and maintaining boundaries ensures that both partners can grow individually while strengthening the relationship.

Steps to Set Healthy Boundaries:

- Define Your Needs: Reflect on what you need to feel safe, supported, and respected in the relationship.
- Communicate Openly: Clearly express your boundaries to your Twin Flame, such as needing time for self-reflection or space to process emotions.
- Respect Mutual Space: Allow each partner time to heal and grow independently, recognizing that periods of separation are often necessary for personal development.

Boundaries foster mutual respect and create a foundation for a healthy, balanced connection.

4. Embracing Detachment and Letting Go of Control

Detachment is one of the most challenging yet crucial aspects of the Twin Flame journey. The intensity of the connection often triggers a desire to control outcomes, but true growth comes from surrendering to the process.

Practices to Cultivate Detachment:

- Surrender Meditation: Visualize yourself releasing control over the relationship. Affirm, "I trust that everything is unfolding as it should."
- Letting Go Rituals: Write down fears or expectations and release them by burning the paper (in a safe setting).
- Trust in Divine Timing: Remind yourself that the Twin Flame journey operates on a higher plane, guided by divine intelligence.

Letting go of control allows love to flow freely and authentically, creating space for spiritual growth.

5. Engaging in Self-Care and Energy Healing

The emotional intensity of a Twin Flame relationship can take a toll on your well-being. Prioritizing self-care and energy healing helps maintain balance and replenishes your physical, emotional, and spiritual reserves.

Self-Care Practices for Twin Flames:

- Physical Activity: Exercise regularly to release tension and improve mood. Activities like yoga or walking in nature can

be particularly grounding.
- Energy Healing: Explore Reiki, crystal healing, or chakra balancing to clear energetic blockages and restore harmony.
- Self-Compassion: Practice kindness toward yourself during challenging moments. Affirm, "I am worthy of love and healing."

Self-care not only nurtures your well-being but also strengthens your ability to engage meaningfully in the relationship.

6. Practicing Forgiveness and Acceptance

Forgiveness is a cornerstone of the Twin Flame journey. Given the mirroring effect of these relationships, misunderstandings and emotional wounds are common. Embracing forgiveness allows for healing and deeper connection.

Steps to Practice Forgiveness:

- Reflect on the Purpose: Recognize that challenges with your Twin Flame serve a higher purpose in your growth.
- Ho'oponopono Prayer: Repeat the phrases, "I'm sorry, please forgive me, thank you, I love you," to release resentment and invite healing.
- Release Judgment: Accept both yourself and your Twin Flame with compassion, understanding that imperfections are part of the human experience.

Forgiveness dissolves negative energy, paving the way for

unconditional love and harmony.

7. Aligning with a Shared Purpose

Many Twin Flame relationships are guided by a shared sense of purpose or mission. Aligning with this purpose can provide direction, deepen the bond, and channel the connection's trans formative energy into meaningful action.

Steps to Discover and Align with a Shared Purpose:

- Reflect on Common Values: Identify values and passions that resonate with both partners.
- Explore Collaborative Goals: Consider how you can work together to uplift others, whether through creative projects, service, or spiritual teaching.
- Stay Open to Evolution: Allow your shared purpose to evolve as you grow individually and together.

A shared purpose transforms the Twin Flame connection into a source of positive impact, enriching both partners and their wider community.

Embracing the Dynamics of the Twin Flame Journey

Navigating a Twin Flame relationship is a deeply personal and spiritual journey. By embracing self-awareness, emotional balance, and spiritual alignment, individuals can transform challenges into profound opportunities for growth.

The Twin Flame path is not merely about union or separation but about awakening to one's highest self and discovering the trans formative power of love. By approaching the journey with patience, compassion, and trust, you honor the sacred purpose of this extraordinary connection.

Key Takeaways

- Reflect on tools such as self-awareness, boundaries, and detachment.
- Consider how these practices can help you navigate complex relationships.

Personal Reflections

1. Which of the tools discussed do you feel is most valuable for you right now? Why?
2. Reflect on a time when setting boundaries or practicing detachment brought clarity to a situation.

Exercises

- Choose one tool (e.g., mindfulness, forgiveness) and commit to practicing it for a week. Journal your experiences and insights.
- Create a self-care plan inspired by the chapter's suggestions.

Closing Thought

"Tools for growth are gifts of self-discovery and empowerment."

6

Lessons from Twin Flames – Soul Evolution and Growth

Journeys of the Heart: Real Stories of Twin Flames and Soul Connections

Twin Flame relationships are often described as profound, life-changing connections that defy ordinary experiences. In this chapter, we explore real-life stories of individuals who have felt the magnetic pull of Twin Flames or soul connections, highlighting the complexity, beauty, and growth these relationships inspire. These narratives offer insights into the transformative power of such bonds, showcasing how they illuminate paths of self-discovery, love, and spiritual evolution.

Diana's Story: A Love Beyond Time

Diana's Twin Flame journey began on her first day of ninth grade—a mix of excitement and apprehension. Entering the shop class, she felt out of place as the only girl, but a boy with gentle green eyes and a calming smile gestured for her to sit beside him. Their connection felt natural, as though they were reuniting rather than meeting for the first time.

Over the weeks, Diana experienced an unexplained pull toward him, but teenage insecurities and peer influences led her to drift away. Despite this, his memory never faded. Decades later, they reunited, and the instant recognition between them reignited the feelings she had suppressed for so long.

Through years of separation, Diana learned patience, self-love, and compassion. Her Twin Flame connection became a lesson in unconditional love—not just for him, but for herself. She now waits with quiet faith, trusting in divine timing to bring them together again.

The Sun and The Moon: A Story of Soul Evolution

Among the profound lessons of the twin flame journey, the experience of *The Sun and The Moon* stands out as a vivid testament to the growth, challenges, and soul-deep transformation that define these connections.

After enduring multiple near-death experiences and defying medical expectations, The Moon, as she called herself, awakened each day with gratitude for God's grace. Her life was dedicated to spiritual growth—seeking divine connection, aligning with the Archangels, and embracing her sacred path. It was during one of her spiritual quests to a distant land, among a group of fellow travelers, that she encountered The Sun.

The moment their eyes met, it was as though her soul recognized his, an inexplicable connection as ancient and profound as the bond between the sun and the moon. Despite her attempts to rationalize it, the magnetic pull was undeniable. The Sun seemed to feel it too, as they found themselves drawn together, engaging in casual conversation that barely scratched the surface of the depth they both felt.

On a remote, mystical island known for its spiritual energy, The Sun approached her with two handcrafted bracelets he had purchased from the local artisans. Gifting her one, he declared, "You are mine now." As his hand covered the bracelet on her wrist, The Moon felt her soul leap forward in recognition. In her mind's eye, a cascade of lifetimes played out like an old film reel—hundreds of incarnations where their lives had intertwined. For a moment, all time and space dissolved as they gazed into each other's souls, an unspoken love and recognition uniting them.

But like many twin flame stories, their connection was not without its challenges. Despite the intensity of their bond, The Sun confessed that he could not risk opening his heart fully. He feared the potential heartbreak if their relationship faltered. The Moon pleaded for him to consider the beauty of trying, of embracing the possibility of divine union over fear of loss. Yet, The Sun's decision was firm.

This rejection felt like a soul-level wound for The Moon—a "soul break" unlike anything she had ever experienced. However, this pain became her greatest teacher. It illuminated the depths of her yearning, not just for her twin flame but for her own growth and alignment with divine will. Through this experience, The Moon learned the profound lesson of surrender: trusting that the divine path would unfold as it was meant to, even if it meant walking it alone.

The story of *The Sun and The Moon* encapsulates the essence of twin flame connections: the deep recognition, the joy of soul reunion, and the inevitable challenges that demand growth and surrender. While their union was fleeting, it was transformative, catalyzing The Moon's spiritual evolution and teaching her the art of releasing control. Through this experience, she came to embody the resilience, love, and surrender that characterize the twin flame journey.

Mara and Caleb: A Connection Beyond Boundaries

Meeting later in life, Mara and Caleb found themselves inextricably drawn to each other despite being married to others. Their bond, intense and undeniable, challenged their commitments and forced them to confront their truths. Choosing to honor their respective marriages, they remained apart but continued to support each other from a distance.

Their connection was a lesson in surrender, teaching Mara to respect the boundaries of love while embracing the personal growth their bond inspired. For her, the Twin Flame journey became a path of honoring love in all its forms, even when it could not be fully realized.

Lucas and Aiden: Cycles of Growth

From the moment they met in college, Lucas and Aiden felt a

fated connection. Their relationship cycled through phases of union and separation, each time bringing both joy and pain. The intensity of their bond forced them to confront unresolved traumas and mirror each other's strengths and wounds.

Through therapy and spiritual guidance, they learned to navigate the challenges of their Twin Flame relationship, transforming their dynamic into one of mutual healing and growth. Over time, Lucas and Aiden embraced their bond as a partnership rooted in love and shared evolution.

Isabella and Raphael: A Spiritual Partnership

Meeting at a meditation retreat, Isabella and Raphael felt a connection that transcended words. Both on spiritual journeys, they discovered a bond more akin to a merging of souls than a romantic attraction. Their partnership became a pillar of support, fostering individual growth and shared purpose.

For Isabella and Raphael, the Twin Flame experience was not defined by romance but by companionship and unconditional love. They reminded each other that true Twin Flame connections can manifest as friendships, alliances, or shared missions, rather than conventional relationships.

Laurora: A Love That Transcends Time

Laurora met her Twin Flame over three decades ago—a connection she describes as "of the stars." Though circumstances kept them from being married in this lifetime, their love has remained unwavering. Their bond, marked by telepathy and an unbreakable spiritual tether, has been a source of strength and grounding for both.

Laurora's journey is a testament to the eternal nature of Twin Flame connections. Despite arguments and separations, their bond has endured, transcending the limitations of time and space. Designing a tattoo for her Twin Flame, a Black Swan, Laurora honors their rare and transformative connection as one that lasts beyond lifetimes.

Grace's Story: The Dance of Reunion and Separation

Grace met her Twin Flame in 2009 when she stepped into his role at work. Their connection was instant and profound, growing through long conversations and shared activities. Despite their bond, conflicting energies and life circumstances created cycles of separation.

Over time, Grace found herself in the roles of both runner and chaser, navigating the complexities of their connection. Though the relationship brought heartache, it also fostered profound personal growth, creativity, and self-awareness. Grace views her journey as far from over, embracing the paradox of holding on while letting go.

Lessons from These Journeys

The stories of Diana, Moon, Mara, Lucas, Isabella, Laurora, and Grace reveal the multifaceted nature of twin flame and soul connections. Each journey is unique, yet they share common themes that illuminate the essence of these relationships. From profound joy to soul-deep pain, these connections challenge, inspire, and transform in ways that defy ordinary human experiences.:

1.The Power of Recognition
Whether it's Diana's instantaneous familiarity or The
Moon's soul-level recognition of The Sun, these
connections often begin with a profound sense of
"knowing." This recognition transcends time, space,
and logic, igniting a connection that feels ancient
and eternal. It serves as a reminder of the soul's
deep wisdom and its yearning for reunion and growth.

2.Self-Discovery and Growth
Each story demonstrates how twin flame relationships
act as mirrors, revealing hidden truths and aspects
of ourselves that demand healing and acceptance. For
The Moon, the intense connection with The Sun
unearthed her unquenchable yearning for divine union,
ultimately leading her to greater self-awareness and
spiritual surrender.

3.Surrender and Faith
As seen in The Sun and The Moon and Mara's story,
surrender is a cornerstone of the twin flame journey.
Both individuals faced the challenge of letting
go--accepting that not all connections will
materialize as we hope, but trusting in the divine
wisdom that guides their path. The act of surrender
teaches resilience and invites us to align with the
greater purpose of the connection, even in separation.

4.The Agony of Separation
Separation, whether by choice, circumstances, or
emotional barriers, is a defining feature of many
twin flame stories. The Moon's "soul break" upon The
Sun's refusal to embrace their connection echoes the

44

deep pain of such moments. Yet, this pain serves a higher purpose, catalyzing profound growth, healing, and the rediscovery of inner strength.

5.Love Beyond Romance
Not all twin flame connections are meant to culminate in romantic union, as Isabella and Raphael's friendship and The Sun and The Moon's fleeting encounter illustrate. The essence of these connections lies not in traditional notions of love but in the spiritual lessons and transformative growth they inspire.

6.Acceptance of Divine Timing
Trusting the timing of the universe is a recurring theme in these journeys. Whether it's Diana's quiet faith in eventual reunion or The Moon's realization that her path would unfold as divinely intended, these stories underscore the importance of patience and trust in a higher plan.

7.Unconditional Love and Forgiveness
Twin flame relationships often demand the deepest levels of compassion and forgiveness--toward both the other person and oneself. For The Moon, her journey with The Sun illuminated the profound lesson of loving without attachment and forgiving the heartbreak caused by fear and uncertainty.

Conclusion: The Soul's Infinite Journey

The stories in this chapter illustrate the transformative power of Twin Flame relationships, highlighting their capacity to inspire growth, healing, and self-realization. Each connection, whether romantic, platonic, or spiritual, serves as a profound step in the soul's journey toward wholeness and love.

For those navigating their own Twin Flame paths, these narratives offer a reminder that the journey is as much about self-discovery as it is about connection. Through the challenges of separation, the joy of reunion, and the lessons of surrender, these relationships guide us toward a deeper understanding of ourselves and the divine love that connects us all.

Key Takeaways

- Reflect on the stories of Twin Flame connections and the lessons they impart.
- Consider how these narratives resonate with your journey.

Personal Reflections

1. Which story from this chapter resonated with you most? Why?
2. Reflect on a lesson you've learned from a deep connection in your life.

Exercises

- Write your own "soul connection" story, highlighting the lessons and growth it brought.
- Create an affirmation inspired by the chapter, focusing on surrender, faith, and self-discovery.

Closing Thought

"Our soul's evolution is written in the stories we live and share."

7

Is God my Twin Flame?

The question "Is God my twin flame?" invites a profound exploration into the spiritual notion that if we are made in God's image, our most intimate and divine relationship may, in fact, be with the Divine itself. In many spiritual traditions, there is an idea that our deepest connection, the one that drives us toward truth, love, and self-realization, could be a reflection of God within us. So, if we are crafted in the image of God, could God be the ultimate "mirror" of our soul—the archetype of the twin flame?

Exploring the Concept

Twin flames are often described as mirrors, reflecting both our light and shadow, challenging us, and urging us to grow. In this context, God, seen as the source of all love and light, could serve as the ultimate mirror. The intense longing, deep love, and sometimes painful growth associated with twin flame relationships might reflect a yearning to reconnect with the Divine essence within us, a reunion with the Source that created us.

Arguments in Favor of the Idea

1. **Oneness and Divine Reflection**:

○ If God created us in His image, then perhaps our most profound twin flame

connection could be with God, who embodies the highest version of ourselves.

This idea aligns with the spiritual notion that the Divine lives within each of us as

our truest self.

2. **The Search for Wholeness**:

○ Twin flames are often described as two halves of one soul. Likewise, many

religious traditions describe humanity as separate from God but eternally seeking

reunion. The intense journey of a twin flame could symbolize humanity's desire to

reunite with God, its other half, on a soul level.

3. **Growth, Healing, and Divine Purpose**:

○ The purpose of a twin flame is not just romance but deep personal growth, healing, and the realization of purpose. If God is our twin flame, our "relationship" with God could be viewed as our ultimate life's purpose: healing, growing, and aligning with our higher selves as reflections of God's image.

Arguments Against the Idea

1. **Twin Flames as Separate Entities**:

○ Traditionally, twin flames are understood as separate souls mirroring each other. If

God is the Creator, it could be argued that God is fundamentally different from an

individual twin flame, as God is whole and complete, while twin flames are two

49

parts seeking completeness.

2 .**Human Limitation in Comprehending Divine Union**:

○ Some might argue that viewing God as a twin flame limits our understanding of

God's boundless nature. Twin flame relationships, with their complexities, may

not fully encompass the transcendental, unconditional nature of God's love, which

is beyond human relationships.

Reflection: Is Seeking God as a Twin Flame Misplaced?

While the twin flame journey teaches self-awareness and the search for divine love, the concept of God as a twin flame encourages us to ponder whether the ultimate "twin flame" is our search for divine union. Perhaps God is not our twin flame in the literal sense, but the longing we feel in life—for connection, truth, and completion—could be a call to discover God's reflection within ourselves. In this way, the journey toward God might resemble the twin flame journey, with God as the destination rather than the flame itself. This concept brings new layers to the twin flame discussion, blending spirituality and self-inquiry, and prompting us to consider that our truest twin flame might be the divine essence within.

Monadic Relationships: A Journey of Inner Unity and Divine Connection

When exploring the realm of soul connections, there's often a fascination with twin flames—the idea of two halves of the same soul, drawn together for spiritual growth, intense love, and transformation. Yet, twin flames are not the only spiritual bond that exists. Another, lesser-known type is the Monadic relationship. Rooted in the idea of monads or individual divine sparks, Monadic relationships emphasize inner unity and divine connection rather than intense mirroring. While twin flame relationships are characterized by a dynamic interplay between two separate yet interconnected souls, Monadic relationships focus on an individual's alignment with their true self and the divine essence within. This chapter delves into what Monadic relationships are, their unique qualities, and how they offer a different but profound path of love and unity.

Understanding Monadic Relationships

The term "Monadic" originates from the Greek word "monas," meaning "one" or "unity." Monadic relationships, then, are relationships rooted in the concept of oneness rather than separation or duality. In these relationships, individuals don't seek a counterpart to complete them. Instead, they are focused on experiencing wholeness and unity within themselves and with the Divine.

In a Monadic relationship, there is no Runner-Chaser dynamic, no intense emotional conflicts, or externalized mirroring. Instead, it is about cultivating inner peace, self-awareness, and a relationship with one's own divine nature. Monadic relationships remind us that we are already complete beings, reflecting our own divine nature rather than seeking it in another.

Key Qualities of Monadic Relationships

Monadic relationships carry distinct qualities that set them apart from twin flame connections:

1. **Inner Wholeness**:

○ In Monadic relationships, the primary focus is on self-unity rather than finding

51

one's "other half." The individual is encouraged to look inward, discover their

divine essence, and cultivate an internal sense of completeness.

2. **Divine Connection**:

◦ Rather than focusing on a person outside oneself, Monadic relationships

emphasize connecting with the Divine. This relationship is often described as an

unshakable sense of unity with the Source, God, or Universal Energy.

3. **Non-Attachment and Unconditional Love**:

◦ Monadic relationships promote a sense of non-attachment, allowing individuals to

love freely without expectation or desire for possession. Love in this relationship

is based on freedom, acceptance, and non-judgment.

4. **Peaceful Self-Realization**:

◦ The Monadic path is often a gentler journey than the twin flame journey, free

from the intense emotional upheaval or painful separations common in twin flame

dynamics. Instead, it promotes steady self-awareness, inner peace, and

harmonious self-realization.

Monadic Relationships vs. Twin Flame Relationships

To understand the contrasts, it helps to look at Monadic and twin flame relationships side by side.

Aspect Twin Flame Relationship Monadic Relationship Focus The "other" as a mirror for growth Self and divine connec-

52

tion

Nature Intense, emotional, often turbulent Peaceful, centered, self-contained

Purpose Growth through duality and mirroring Self-unity and alignment with Divine

Dynamic Runner-Chaser, emotional triggers No chasing, focused on inner wholeness

Love Style Often includes attachment, intense passion, Unconditional, non-attached, rooted in acceptance

Challenges Emotional upheaval, healing past wounds Developing self-awareness and nurturing self-love

The Spiritual Purpose of Monadic Relationships

Monadic relationships are a pathway to divine connection. In contrast to the mirroring that happens in twin flame relationships, where another person reflects both positive and negative aspects of oneself, Monadic relationships are about understanding that the Divine already exists within. This realization transforms one's relationship with themselves, with others, and with the world.1

. **Personal Spiritual Growth**:

○ A Monadic relationship encourages individuals to align with their inner truth,

values, and sense of purpose. This process can be deeply trans formative, but it

often lacks the emotional turbulence typical of twin flame experiences.

2. **Healing Through Self-Acceptance**:

○ While twin flame relationships often involve healing through external conflict,

Monadic relationships promote healing through acceptance and understanding.

53

The individual learns to embrace their full self—flaws and all—without seeking
external validation.

3. Embracing Divine Oneness:

○ In Monadic relationships, the individual comes to experience divine love and
oneness firsthand. This is a love that transcends individual personality and ego,
revealing an eternal connection to the divine source.

Exercises for Embracing a Monadic Relationship

Here are practices to help readers explore and deepen their Monadic connection with themselves and the Divine.

Meditation on Inner Unity

- **Purpose**: This meditation allows readers to experience a sense of inner wholeness.
- **Instructions**: 1. 2. 3. 4. Sit comfortably, close your eyes, and take a few deep breaths. Visualize a bright light at your heart center, growing with each inhale. Imagine this light expanding to fill your entire body, creating a warm, radiant sense of wholeness and unity. Repeat silently, "I am whole. I am complete. I am one with the Divine."

Affirmations for Self-Unity

- Using affirmations can reinforce self-love and acceptance, two pillars of Monadic

relationships.

- **Affirmations**:

54

- ○ "I am whole and complete within myself."
- ○ "I connect with the divine essence within me."
- ○ "I am love, I am peace, I am unity."

Journaling Exercise: Connecting with the Divine

- **Prompt**: Reflect on your relationship with the divine essence within you. Write down any ways in which you feel connected to or disconnected from your inner divine self.
- **Goal**: This exercise helps readers to explore their own feelings about divine love and unity, fostering a Monadic relationship.

Embracing both paths while Monadic relationships and twin flame relationships may seem different, they both lead toward the same ultimate goal: spiritual growth, love, and self-actualization. Some may experience a twin flame connection, while others may walk a Monadic path, finding love and unity within themselves. The key is to remember that both relationships are sacred in their own right. Whether through a twin flame or a Monadic journey, the destination remains the same: the discovery of love, peace, and unity within.

Key Takeaways

- Reflect on the idea of God as the ultimate mirror or twin flame.
- Explore how divine love may serve as a guiding force in your journey.

Personal Reflections

1. How does the concept of divine love as a Twin Flame resonate with your spiritual beliefs?
2. Reflect on moments when you felt deeply connected to a higher power.

Exercises

- Write a prayer or meditation asking for guidance in deepening your connection with the Divine.
- Journal about how cultivating a relationship with the Divine has impacted your life.

Closing Thought
"Divine love is the flame that illuminates our path."

8

Mirror, Mirror on the Wall: Am I My Twin Flame After All?

The Twin Flame journey is intimately tied to the concept of reflection. We often think of our Twin Flame as someone who mirrors our innermost emotions, fears, dreams, and potential. This person holds up a mirror to our soul, allowing us to see ourselves with unparalleled clarity. But what if, on a deeper level, we are our own Twin Flame? Could the ultimate purpose of this journey be to recognize and embrace our inherent wholeness within ourselves?

In this chapter, we will explore the trans formative concept of becoming our own Twin Flame. We will delve into the role of self-reflection and self-acceptance, the importance of harmonizing light and shadow, and how cultivating a loving relationship with ourselves may unlock the true potential of a Twin Flame connection.

The Twin Flame as a Mirror of the Self

At its core, the Twin Flame connection is often described as a mirror—a perfect reflection of our strengths, vulnerabilities, and untapped potential. These relationships bring hidden aspects of ourselves to the surface, encouraging us to confront and embrace parts we may have neglected or feared.

However, these reflections are not solely about what we need to change. They are invitations to embrace our authentic selves more fully. The Twin Flame dynamic can blur the boundaries between self and other, raising a profound question: Are the reflections we see in our Twin Flame merely aspects of ourselves waiting to be acknowledged and loved?

If so, then finding wholeness within may be the first step toward experiencing true Twin Flame union.

Embracing Self-Love as the Foundation of Twin Flame Union

In the search for a Twin Flame, many people feel a deep longing for completion, believing that their Twin holds the missing piece to their soul. Yet, the journey often reveals that no one else can complete us. The power to discover our wholeness lies within.

Self-love is not only a prerequisite for a healthy Twin Flame relationship—it is the foundation of true, lasting fulfillment. By cultivating deep love and respect for ourselves, we align with the energy we wish to experience in our external relationships. Viewing ourselves as worthy, whole, and lovable allows us to radiate a frequency that attracts authentic love both within and beyond.

Practical Steps to Cultivate Self-Love

1. Mirror Work: Stand before a mirror and look deeply into your eyes. Speak affirmations such as, "I am worthy," "I am whole," and "I am enough." This practice may feel challenging at first, but over time, it fosters acceptance and compassion.

2. Gratitude Journal for the Self: Each day, write down qualities you admire about yourself. Celebrate both achievements and inner strengths to build a reservoir of self-appreciation.

3. Practice Forgiveness: Release self-judgment and regret through journaling or meditation. Offer yourself the compassion you would extend to a loved one.

Self-love is the gateway to realizing that we are, in many ways, our own Twin Flame. By loving ourselves unconditionally, we transcend the need for external validation and discover true wholeness.

Understanding Inner Union: Balancing Masculine and Feminine Energies

The Twin Flame journey often speaks of the "divine masculine" and "divine feminine" energies. These energies are not tied to gender but represent aspects of consciousness that exist within each of us. The masculine energy embodies logic, action, and strength, while the feminine energy represents intuition, compassion, and creativity.

Achieving balance between these energies, or "inner union," is a vital step in the Twin Flame path. By harmonizing these aspects within ourselves, we create a sense of inner completeness and embody the unity we seek externally.

Exercises for Balancing Masculine and Feminine Energies

1. Creative Expression: Engage in intuitive activities such as painting, journaling, or dancing to awaken your feminine energy.
2. Goal-Setting and Action Planning: Focus on structure and discipline by setting clear goals and working toward them, activating your masculine energy.
3. Meditative Visualization: Envision the masculine and feminine energies within you merging in harmony, creating a balanced state of inner peace.

When we achieve inner balance, we reflect the essence of the Twin Flame connection—a unity that honors all aspects of our being.

Embracing Both Light and Shadow

The Twin Flame journey is renowned for uncovering shadow aspects of the self—those parts we deny or fear. Shadow work can be difficult, as it requires confronting insecurities, past wounds, and fears. However, embracing our shadow is a crucial step toward self-acceptance and inner peace.

Shadow Work Practices

1. Journaling Your Fears: Write down your insecurities and limiting beliefs. Examine their origins and their impact on your life.
2. Dialogue with Your Inner Child: Visualize comforting your inner child, offering them love and reassurance.
3. Non-Judgmental Awareness: When faced with challenging emotions, observe them without criticism. Remind yourself that imperfection is part of being human.

By integrating our shadow with our light, we create a foundation of unconditional self-acceptance. This wholeness allows us to approach all relationships, including a Twin Flame connection, with authenticity and strength.

The Journey of Self-Realization: Becoming Whole

The essence of the Twin Flame journey is the realization that we are already complete. Becoming our own Twin Flame means finding wholeness within and embracing all parts of ourselves—light and shadow, masculine and feminine.

This perspective does not diminish the potential for an external Twin Flame relationship but enriches it. Approaching such a connection from a place of inner wholeness releases dependency and fear, transforming love into a sacred choice rather than a need.

Meditation: Visualizing Your Inner Twin Flame

1. Close Your Eyes: Take a few deep breaths, centering

yourself in the present moment.

2. See a Mirror: Visualize a mirror reflecting not just your physical form but your soul's essence.

3. Meet Your Inner Twin: See your Twin Flame in the mirror, representing all the love and potential within you.

4. Merge with the Reflection: Imagine dissolving into the reflection, affirming your wholeness.

5. Affirm Your Completeness: Conclude with, "I am whole. I am my own Twin Flame. I am complete within myself."

This meditation fosters a sense of unity within, reminding you that you already carry the qualities of a Twin Flame.

Re imagining the Twin Flame Journey

When we consider the possibility that we are our own Twin Flame, the journey takes on a deeper, more personal meaning. Instead of seeking completion in another, we honor the completeness that has always existed within.

By cultivating self-love, balancing our inner energies, embracing our shadow, and realizing our wholeness, we unlock the potential for true Twin Flame union—not only with another person but within the sacred union of our own soul.

Key Takeaways

· Reflect on the concept of becoming your own Twin Flame.
· Explore how self-love and balance lead to inner union.

Personal Reflections

1. How do you currently practice self-love? How might you deepen this practice?
2. Reflect on how balancing your inner energies has impacted your growth.

Exercises

- Create a self-love ritual, such as daily affirmations or a gratitude journal for yourself.
- Write about the qualities you see in your Twin Flame and how you might cultivate them within yourself.

Closing Thought

"The ultimate union is the one we create within."

9

Healthy or Toxic? Examining the Twin Flame Relationship

In the pursuit of a soul-deep, unconditionally loving relationship, many individuals seek the ultimate connection—a Twin Flame, their other half, the one person who completes their soul. This concept has inspired people to search fervently, convinced that finding their Twin Flame will bring life-changing love and fulfillment. When individuals believe they have found their Twin Flame, the connection can feel incredibly powerful, often rooted in shared experiences or past traumas that create an intense bond. This connection can feel so unique and consuming that it convinces people they have found the one who mirrors their soul, creating a sense that they are two halves of the same whole.

However, this deep sense of connection and familiarity raises the question: is this intense bond healthy or toxic? Some individuals cling to the Twin Flame ideology, using it to excuse or overlook troubling behavior within the relationship. They believe that enduring hardships and pain will eventually bring about unity and oneness. But in a truly healthy relationship, love does not require constant pain or abuse, nor does it demand one to endure harmful behavior in the hope of eventual harmony. Instead, love seeks to support, uplift, and protect without causing intentional harm.

The Netflix documentary *Twin Flames Universe* highlights the extremes some people will go to in the name of finding and keeping their Twin Flame. The documentary exposes cases where individuals were advised to change their gender identity to fit the idea of an "approved Twin Flame" or were instructed to endure abusive behavior from someone deemed their Twin Flame by the organization. This manipulation preyed on people's vulnerabilities, exploiting their longing for love and connection. It's disturbing to see individuals manipulated into tolerating or even accepting behavior that harms them physically, mentally, or emotionally, all under the guise of "true love."

As heartbreaking as it is, such examples are not unique to one organization. Many so-called "Twin Flame experts" have created frameworks that encourage seekers to endure toxic relationships in the name of spiritual growth. This includes telling individuals to disregard boundaries, ignore red flags, or tolerate mistreatment in the hope that their patience will be rewarded with ultimate union. Such teachings pervert the essence of love, turning what should be an uplifting connection into a harmful cycle of dependence, pain, and control.

When we consider the religious teachings that emphasize love, respect, and mutual care, it becomes clear that the Twin Flame Universe's approach, and others like it, diverge sharply from true spiritual principles. The Bible speaks of the selfless love a partner should have, where each person places the other's well-being above their own and refrains from using force or causing harm. True love, as described in Ephesians 5:25-33 and Corinthians 13:4-7, is patient, kind, and respectful. Love is meant to lift and protect, not to break down or exploit. By this definition, a relationship that requires enduring abuse or manipulation cannot be considered truly loving or healthy.

The Twin Flame ideology has captivated many in the spiritual community, leading to the emergence of countless "experts" who claim to have the authority to guide individuals in their Twin Flame journey. Yet, psychology often views relationships characterized by extreme highs and lows, constant running and chasing, or cycles of harm and reconciliation as unhealthy. Terms like "trauma bonding," "narcissistic abuse," "codependency," and "gaslighting" come into play in these dynamics, and they are signs that the relationship may be toxic rather than divinely inspired.

Some spiritual teachers may romanticize these unhealthy relationships, asserting that enduring and mastering such hardships leads to personal growth and spiritual expansion. But this view can dangerously justify or normalize harmful behavior. When people allow themselves to be mistreated under the guise of spiritual growth, they often lose touch with their self-worth, compromise their mental health, and, in some cases, put themselves in physical danger. For instance, people have committed illegal acts like stalking or harassing their perceived Twin Flame, convinced that these actions were part of their "destined journey." This is not love but rather an unhealthy attachment that obscures the true purpose of relationships: mutual support and respect.

In the pursuit of a Twin Flame, some individuals may isolate themselves, dismissing healthy relationships or support systems in favor of this single, intense bond. They might cling

66

to the belief that overcoming obstacles will eventually bring them ultimate love, even if it means suffering. However, it is essential to distinguish between normal relationship challenges and patterns of harm. While no relationship is without its struggles, enduring continuous pain or unhealthy behavior as part of a supposed spiritual test or journey often points to deeper issues that need attention beyond the relationship itself. True love does not require endless suffering or sacrifice but instead seeks to nurture, grow, and empower each individual.

For those grappling with the intensity of a Twin Flame relationship, it may be beneficial to seek guidance from a licensed therapist or counselor. These professionals can provide clarity, helping individuals discern whether their relationship is nurturing or toxic. Therapy can help uncover any patterns of dependence, past traumas, or emotional wounds that might be clouding one's judgment. This kind of self-awareness is essential for personal growth and for cultivating relationships that are genuinely loving and supportive.

In summary, while the idea of a Twin Flame offers a captivating image of deep connection and unconditional love, it is crucial to approach this concept with caution. No relationship should demand the sacrifice of one's well-being, integrity, or self-respect. True love is based on mutual respect, understanding, and a desire to help each other grow in a healthy way. If a Twin Flame relationship strays from these principles, it may be time to reevaluate its place in one's life and to focus on self-love and healing. After all, a loving, supportive relationship begins within oneself.

Key Takeaways

- Reflect on the characteristics of healthy versus toxic relationships.
- Consider how the Twin Flame concept can sometimes blur these boundaries.

Personal Reflections

1. How do you differentiate between challenges that foster growth and patterns that harm?
2. Reflect on the health of your relationships. What changes, if any, might you need to make?

Exercises

- Create a list of red flags and green flags for relationships in your life.
- Write a letter to yourself affirming your commitment to healthy and nurturing relationships.

Closing Thought
"True love uplifts, nurtures, and inspires growth."

10

Healing and Moving Forward

The Twin Flame journey is a deeply trans formative experience, often marked by periods of intense connection, separation, and self-discovery. While the connection itself can be exhilarating, the path is not always smooth. Separation, emotional triggers, and unresolved wounds can leave individuals grappling with feelings of loss, confusion, and even despair.

However, the journey also offers immense opportunities for healing and growth. By embracing these moments with courage and intention, individuals can emerge with a stronger sense of self, deeper clarity, and the ability to move forward—whether toward reunion or a new chapter of life.

This chapter provides tools, practices, and perspectives to aid in the healing process and help balance the intensity of the Twin Flame connection with a fulfilling and independent life.

The Importance of Healing in the Twin Flame Journey

Healing is at the heart of the Twin Flame experience. The challenges and triggers that arise within the connection are not merely obstacles but opportunities to address unresolved emotions, release limiting beliefs, and align with one's authentic self.

Key Aspects of Healing:

1. Emotional Processing: Allowing yourself to feel and work through emotions rather than suppressing them.
2. Inner Child Work: Addressing wounds and unmet needs from childhood that may influence relationship patterns.
3. Self-Love: Cultivating a deep sense of worth and compassion for yourself, independent of external validation.
4. Spiritual Growth: Using the challenges of the journey to deepen your connection with your higher self and the Divine.

Healing is not only essential for the individual but also creates the foundation for a balanced and harmonious Twin Flame relationship, should reunion occur.

Methods for Healing After Separation

Separation from a Twin Flame can be one of the most challenging aspects of the journey. While it may feel like a loss, it often serves as a necessary phase for individual growth and self-realization.

Strategies for Healing During Separation:

- Journaling: Reflect on your emotions, lessons, and personal growth through writing. Explore questions like, "What am I learning from this experience?"
- Meditation and Mindfulness: Practice staying present with your feelings without judgment. Techniques such as breath work or guided meditations can bring calm and clarity.
- Energy Healing: Engage in practices like Reiki, chakra balancing, or sound healing to release energetic blockages and restore harmony.
- Creative Expression: Channel your emotions into art, music, or writing to process and transform them into something meaningful.

Separation is not the end of the journey but an opportunity to cultivate resilience, independence, and self-love.

Detachment with Love

One of the most profound lessons of the Twin Flame journey is learning to detach with love. Detachment does not mean abandoning the connection but rather releasing expectations and control. This creates space for authentic growth and alignment with the divine timing of the journey.

Practices for Detachment:

- Surrender Visualization: Imagine releasing the energetic ties of attachment, affirming, "I trust that what is meant for me will come in its perfect time."
- Affirmations: Repeat affirmations such as, "I am whole and

complete within myself," to reinforce independence and
inner peace.

- Focus on the Present: Redirect energy toward personal
  goals, hobbies, and relationships that bring joy and fulfillment.

Detachment with love allows you to honor the connection while
prioritizing your own healing and well-being.

Balancing the Twin Flame Journey with Independence

While the Twin Flame journey is deeply trans formative, it is
essential to maintain a sense of individuality and balance. The
relationship should complement your life, not consume it.

Ways to Cultivate Balance:

1. Set Boundaries: Ensure that your needs, goals, and personal growth remain a priority.
2. Invest in Self-Care: Regularly engage in practices that
   nurture your physical, emotional, and spiritual health.
3. Build a Support System: Connect with friends, family,
   or spiritual communities who can provide guidance and
   encouragement.
4. Pursue Personal Passions: Focus on hobbies, career aspira-
   tions, or creative projects that bring you joy and purpose.

By fostering independence, you create a strong foundation for
personal growth and ensure that your journey remains aligned

with your highest self.

Moving Forward After a Twin Flame Connection

Not all Twin Flame journeys lead to reunion, and for some, the connection serves as a powerful but temporary catalyst for growth. Whether or not union occurs, the lessons and transformations gained from the experience are invaluable.

Steps for Moving Forward:

- Embrace the Lessons: Reflect on the insights and growth the connection has brought into your life.
- Focus on Gratitude: Appreciate the beauty and intensity of the journey, even if it was challenging.
- Create a Vision for the Future: Envision a life filled with purpose, joy, and love, independent of the Twin Flame connection.
- Stay Open to New Connections: Trust that your path will continue to bring meaningful relationships and experiences.

Moving forward is not about forgetting the connection but about integrating its lessons and embracing the next phase of your journey with openness and trust.

Healing as a Lifelong Journey

Healing within the Twin Flame journey is not a one-time event but an ongoing process. Each phase of the relationship offers new opportunities for growth and self-discovery. By committing to healing as a lifelong journey, you cultivate a deeper connection with yourself and the Divine.

Continual Practices for Healing:

- Daily Reflection: Set aside time each day to journal, meditate, or practice gratitude.
- Seek Guidance: Consider working with a mentor, counselor, or spiritual teacher to support your journey.
- Celebrate Progress: Acknowledge and honor the strides you have made in your healing and growth.

Healing allows you to step into your highest potential, whether or not your Twin Flame journey continues.

Embracing the Journey

The Twin Flame journey is as much about self-discovery and healing as it is about love and connection. By facing the challenges with courage, embracing the lessons with an open heart, and prioritizing your well-being, you honor the trans formative power of this extraordinary experience.

Whether you find yourself reunited with your Twin Flame or embarking on a new chapter of life, the growth and insights you have gained will serve as a foundation for a brighter, more authentic future.

Spiritual Practices for Alignment and Healing

For many, the twin flame journey is not only about love but

spiritual evolution. Here are spiritual practices to help readers grow and heal on this journey.

Self-Compassion Practice

- Purpose: Cultivating self-compassion is essential for healing wounds and embracing oneself fully.
- Practice:
- Readers can place their hand on their heart and repeat, "I am worthy of love and compassion. I forgive myself for past mistakes, and I release guilt or shame."
- Encourage them to repeat this practice whenever they feel unworthy or unlovable, to reconnect with their divine nature.

Chakra Balancing for Emotional and Spiritual Alignment

- Purpose: Chakra balancing can help clear energy blockages often activated by twin flame interactions, especially in the heart (for love), solar plexus (personal power), and root (stability) chakras.
- Practice:
- ○ Visualize light or energy flowing through each chakra, starting at the root and moving up to the crown.
- ○ Encourage readers to focus on the heart chakra, imagining it as a radiant green light, as they repeat affirmations of love and compassion.

Energy Cord Cutting Ritual

- Purpose: Sometimes, to maintain peace, one may need to

release attachments while still holding love. This ritual can be used to release excess emotional ties to the twin flame when separation is necessary.

- Instructions:
- ○ Visualize a cord connecting your heart to your twin flame's heart.
- ○ Imagine gently cutting or releasing this cord, affirming, "I release you with love and peace, and I reclaim my energy to focus on my own growth."
- ○ This exercise doesn't sever the bond permanently but creates emotional space for healing.

Key Takeaways

- Reflect on how healing paves the way for new beginnings.
- Consider how forgiveness and letting go can free you for the next phase of your journey.

Personal Reflections

1. What steps have you taken to heal from past relationships? How have they helped you grow?
2. Reflect on how letting go has created space for new possibilities in your life.

Exercises

- Write a letter to a past version of yourself, offering forgiveness and compassion.
- Create a vision board for your healed and empowered future self.

Closing Thought

"Healing is the bridge between who we were and who we are becoming."

11

Embracing the Twin Flame Path

The Twin Flame journey is one of the most trans formative paths a person can undertake. It challenges conventional ideas about love, pushes the boundaries of emotional and spiritual growth, and reveals the depth of human connection. Whether your journey involves reunion, separation, or an entirely different outcome, the lessons learned along the way are invaluable.

The Twin Flame journey is as unique as the individuals who experience it. While common themes and patterns exist, the path is deeply personal, shaped by your soul's purpose and the lessons you are meant to learn.

This chapter is an invitation to embrace your journey in its entirety—the joys, challenges, and everything in between. Whether you are navigating the intensity of union, the solitude of separation, or the balance of self-discovery, know that every step is a sacred part of your evolution.

Honoring Your Experience

Each Twin Flame connection offers invaluable lessons that can transform your understanding of love, self, and the universe. Honoring your experience means recognizing its significance, even in moments of difficulty or uncertainty.

Ways to Honor Your Journey:

- Practice Gratitude: Reflect on the growth and insights you've gained, even from the most challenging phases.
- Acknowledge Your Strength: Celebrate your courage and resilience in facing the intensity of the Twin Flame path.
- Find Meaning in the Challenges: View obstacles as opportunities for growth and transformation.

By honoring your experience, you affirm the importance of your journey and its role in your spiritual evolution.

Letting Go of Comparisons

It's easy to compare your journey to others', especially when engaging with the broader Twin Flame community. However, each connection is unique, and there is no universal timeline or outcome.

How to Release Comparisons:

- Focus on Your Path: Trust that your journey is unfolding exactly as it should for your highest good.
- Embrace Individuality: Recognize that your experiences are tailored to your soul's specific needs and lessons.

79

- Avoid External Validation: Shift your attention from others' opinions to your own inner guidance.

Letting go of comparisons allows you to fully embrace the authenticity and purpose of your journey.

Trusting the Divine Plan

The Twin Flame journey often defies logic and expectations, requiring trust in the unknown. Whether your connection leads to reunion, separation, or something entirely unexpected, trusting the divine plan ensures that you remain open to the possibilities of growth and fulfillment.

Twin Flames as Mirrors of the Soul

At its heart, the Twin Flame journey is about self-discovery. These connections act as mirrors, reflecting both the light and shadow aspects of our souls. By confronting these reflections, individuals are invited to grow, heal, and align with their highest selves.

The journey compels us to:

- Embrace Vulnerability: Allowing ourselves to feel deeply and confront our fears.
- Heal and Integrate: Working through past traumas and achieving a sense of inner wholeness.
- Seek Authenticity: Shedding societal expectations to align with our truest selves.

The Twin Flame connection ultimately serves as a profound reminder of our divine essence and potential.

The Transformative Power of Love

The Twin Flame journey redefines love, moving beyond romantic ideals to encompass unconditional acceptance and compassion. It teaches that love is not about possession or completion but about growth, freedom, and mutual respect.

Key Lessons About Love:

1. Unconditionality: Learning to love oneself and others without conditions or expectations.
2. Interdependence: Balancing deep connection with individual freedom and self-reliance.
3. Divine Love: Recognizing that all love is rooted in a higher, universal force that connects us all.

Through these lessons, the Twin Flame journey expands our capacity to love—not just our Twin Flame, but ourselves and the world around us.

Viewing the Journey as a Tool for Growth

While the Twin Flame connection often evokes intense emotions, it is ultimately a tool for personal and spiritual evolution. The challenges and triumphs experienced along the way serve to align us with our soul's purpose and higher path.

Practical Steps to Embrace Growth:

- Reflect regularly on the lessons the journey has brought into your life.
- Practice gratitude for the experiences that have shaped you, even the painful ones.
- Use the insights gained to create a life aligned with your values, passions, and higher self.

The journey is not about an endpoint but about the transformation that occurs along the way.

Reaffirming Self-Love and Wholeness

A central theme of the Twin Flame experience is the journey toward self-love and inner wholeness. Twin Flames teach us that we are already complete as we are, and that true connection begins within.

Steps to Cultivate Self-Love:

1. Daily Affirmations: Reinforce your worth with affirmations like, "I am whole and worthy of love."
2. Self-Care Practices: Nurture your physical, emotional, and spiritual well-being regularly.
3. Inner Dialogue: Speak to yourself with kindness and compassion, especially during challenging moments.

By embracing self-love, you create a solid foundation for all other connections in your life.

Moving Forward with an Open Heart

Whether your Twin Flame journey results in reunion or separation, it is an opportunity to move forward with greater clarity, strength, and openness. Each phase of the journey is a stepping stone toward a deeper understanding of yourself and the world.

Tips for Moving Forward:

- Stay Open to Possibilities: Trust that your path will continue to bring meaningful experiences and connections.
- Pursue Your Purpose: Align your actions with your soul's calling and focus on creating a life of fulfillment.
- Celebrate Your Growth: Acknowledge how far you've come and the wisdom you've gained along the way.

Moving forward does not mean leaving the connection behind; it means integrating its lessons into a richer, more authentic life.

Embracing the Mystery

The Twin Flame journey is steeped in mystery, defying simple explanations or linear progressions. It is a path that challenges, transforms, and inspires those who walk it.

By embracing the mystery, you allow yourself to remain curious, open, and trusting in the unfolding of your journey. Let the

unknown be a source of wonder rather than fear, and trust that
every step is guided by a higher purpose.

A Journey of Love and Transformation

The Twin Flame journey is not just about a relationship; it is
about awakening to the infinite possibilities of love, growth, and
connection. It teaches us that love is not confined to one person
or moment but is a force that weaves through every aspect of
our lives.

Whether you are just beginning your Twin Flame journey, in
the midst of its intensity, or reflecting on its lessons, remember
that this path is a sacred opportunity to discover your truest
self.

May your journey be one of healing, joy, and transformation,
and may the love you uncover guide you to your highest potential.

Key Takeaways

- Reflect on the transformative nature of the Twin Flame
  journey and how it challenges conventional ideas of love.
- Recognize the unique and sacred nature of your individual
  journey.
- Embrace the lessons learned, whether through joy, challenge, reunion, or separation.

Personal Reflections

1. What has been the most transformative lesson from your journey so far? How has it changed your perspective on love and connection?
2. Reflect on a moment when you felt deeply connected to your Twin Flame path. What emotions or insights emerged?

Exercises

- **Gratitude Practice**: Write down three lessons or experiences from your Twin Flame journey that you are grateful for. How have these moments contributed to your growth?
- **Letting Go Ritual**: Reflect on any comparisons or expectations you may have been holding about your journey. Write them down and release them by tearing the paper or burning it safely, affirming, "My path unfolds perfectly for me."

Self-Discovery Prompts

- In what ways has your Twin Flame connection acted as a mirror for your own growth and healing?
- How have you grown in self-love and self-awareness through this journey? Write about any specific practices that have supported this growth.

Closing Thought

"Embracing the Twin Flame path is a courageous act of honoring love, transformation, and self-discovery. Trust that every step you take is guided by a divine purpose."

12

Frequently Asked Questions About Twin Flames

The Twin Flame journey is deeply personal and often mysterious, leaving many individuals with questions about their experiences. While no two journeys are exactly alike, certain themes and patterns frequently emerge, leading to common inquiries.

This chapter addresses some of the most frequently asked questions about Twin Flames, offering clarity, guidance, and reassurance to those navigating this trans formative path.

1. What exactly is a Twin Flame?

A Twin Flame is often described as the other half of one's soul or as two souls that share the same energetic essence. Twin Flames are believed to reunite in human form to help each other grow, heal, and align with their highest purpose.

Unlike conventional relationships, Twin Flames serve as mirrors, reflecting both the light and shadow aspects of each other. Their connection transcends physical attraction or compatibility, focusing instead on spiritual evolution and transformation.

2. How do I know if I've met my Twin Flame?

Recognizing a Twin Flame often involves a profound sense of familiarity and connection, as though you've known this person across lifetimes. Common signs include:

- Immediate Recognition: Feeling as if you've "come home" upon meeting.
- Intense Emotional Bond: Experiencing heightened emotions, both joyful and challenging.
- Mirroring Dynamics: Noticing that your Twin Flame reflects your inner strengths and vulnerabilities.
- Spiritual Awakening: Feeling inspired to grow, heal, or explore your spirituality.

While these signs can provide clues, the Twin Flame journey is ultimately about personal growth rather than labeling the connection.

3. Are Twin Flames always romantic?

No, Twin Flames are not always romantic. While many Twin Flame connections involve romantic relationships, these bonds can also manifest as deep friendships, familial relationships, or even professional partnerships.

The defining characteristic of a Twin Flame connection is not its romantic nature but its intensity and purpose in fostering spiritual growth.

4. Why do Twin Flames experience separation?

Separation is a common phase in the Twin Flame journey and often serves an essential purpose. It allows both partners to:

- Heal Individually: Address unresolved emotions, traumas, or limiting beliefs.
- Develop Independence: Cultivate self-reliance and a sense of wholeness outside the relationship.
- Align Spiritually: Work on personal growth and align with their higher selves.

While separation can be painful, it is often a necessary step toward healing and eventual reunion.

5. What is the "Runner and Chaser" dynamic?

The "Runner and Chaser" dynamic occurs when one partner (the Runner) withdraws from the relationship due to fear, overwhelm, or unresolved issues, while the other partner (the Chaser) seeks to restore connection.

This dynamic highlights areas where both individuals need healing:

- The Runner: Often fears vulnerability, intimacy, or emo-

tional overwhelm.
- The Chaser: Often struggles with attachment, abandonment fears, or the need for validation.

Resolving this dynamic requires both partners to focus on their individual growth rather than attempting to control or fix the relationship.

6. Can Twin Flames have a harmonious union?

Yes, Twin Flames can achieve a harmonious union, but this often requires significant inner work from both partners. A balanced and healthy Twin Flame relationship is characterized by:

- Mutual Respect: Both partners honor each other's individuality and boundaries.
- Emotional Balance: Each partner has addressed their inner wounds and cultivated self-love.
- Shared Purpose: The relationship aligns with a greater spiritual mission or shared goal.

Harmonious union is less about perfection and more about authenticity, mutual growth, and alignment.

7. What is the difference between a Twin Flame and a Soulmate?

While both Twin Flames and Soulmates represent deep spiritual connections, they serve different purposes:

- Soulmates: These are members of your soul family, such as friends, romantic partners, or mentors. They provide love, support, and companionship but typically do not challenge you as deeply as a Twin Flame.
- Twin Flames: This singular connection serves as a catalyst for profound transformation, requiring both individuals to face their inner truths and evolve spiritually.

In essence, Soulmates comfort and nurture, while Twin Flames challenge and inspire.

8. Is everyone meant to meet their Twin Flame?

Not everyone will encounter their Twin Flame in this lifetime, and that is perfectly okay. The Twin Flame journey is just one of many paths to spiritual growth and self-realization.

For some, their life purpose may focus on other forms of connection, healing, or service. Every journey is unique and equally valuable in the grand scheme of spiritual evolution.

9. What should I do if I believe I've met my Twin Flame?

If you believe you've met your Twin Flame, consider these steps:

- Focus on Self-Growth: Prioritize healing, self-love, and personal development.
- Release Expectations: Avoid trying to control or predict the outcome of the relationship.
- Seek Support: Connect with spiritual mentors, counselors,

or supportive communities.
- Trust the Process: Embrace the journey as it unfolds, trusting that each phase serves a purpose.

Meeting your Twin Flame is not about immediate union but about the lessons and growth the connection inspires.

10. Can Twin Flames be toxic?

While Twin Flame relationships can be intense and challenging, they should not be confused with toxic dynamics. Toxic relationships are characterized by manipulation, control, or abuse, which are not hallmarks of a true Twin Flame connection.

If a relationship feels harmful or draining, it is essential to prioritize your well-being, regardless of its label. True Twin Flame connections foster growth and healing, even in moments of challenge.

11. How can I heal after a Twin Flame separation?

Healing after a Twin Flame separation involves self-care, reflection, and spiritual alignment. Strategies include:

- Practicing Forgiveness: Release resentment toward yourself or your Twin Flame.
- Embracing Self-Love: Cultivate a sense of worth and wholeness independent of the relationship.
- Exploring Your Spiritual Path: Use the separation as an opportunity to deepen your connection with your higher

self.

Separation is not the end of the journey but a chance to grow
stronger and more aligned.

12. What is the ultimate purpose of a Twin Flame connection?

The ultimate purpose of a Twin Flame connection is not romantic fulfillment but spiritual evolution. These relationships
challenge individuals to:

- Heal and Transform: Address unresolved emotions and
  align with their highest selves.
- Discover Their Purpose: Step into their divine calling and
  contribute to the greater good.
- Embody Unconditional Love: Learn to love without conditions, beginning with themselves.

The Twin Flame journey is a sacred path, guiding individuals toward deeper understanding, authenticity, and spiritual growth.

13

Conclusion

The Transformative Power of the Twin Flame Journey

The Twin Flame journey is one of the most profound and trans
formative experiences a soul can undertake. It invites us to
explore the depths of love, face the truths of who we are, and
embrace a path of spiritual evolution. Far beyond the realm of
conventional relationships, Twin Flames challenge us to grow,
heal, and align with our highest selves.

As you navigate your unique path, remember that this journey
is not solely about reunion or the relationship itself—it is about
you. It is about uncovering your own strength, discovering
your divine purpose, and awakening to the infinite possibilities
within and around you.

A Journey of Growth and Healing

Each phase of the Twin Flame connection—whether it involves
joy, pain, union, or separation—serves as a catalyst for personal

and spiritual growth. The challenges you face along the way are
not obstacles but opportunities to heal, transform, and evolve.

Through this journey, you may discover:

- The Power of Self-Love: Learning to embrace yourself as
  whole and worthy, independent of external validation.
- The Beauty of Unconditional Love: Cultivating compassion
  and acceptance for yourself and others.
- The Depth of Your Strength: Overcoming fears, doubts, and
  limitations to align with your highest potential.

By embracing these lessons, you honor the sacred purpose of
the Twin Flame connection.

Trusting the Process

The Twin Flame journey often defies logic and expectations,
requiring patience, trust, and surrender. While the path may
not always be clear, each step brings you closer to a deeper
understanding of yourself and your soul's purpose.

Key Reminders:

- You Are Not Alone: Many others share similar experiences,
  and their stories can provide inspiration and encouragement.
- Everything Is Divinely Timed: Trust that the journey unfolds exactly as it should, in alignment with your highest
  good.

94

- Your Growth Matters Most: The ultimate purpose of the journey is your personal evolution and self-realization.

Trusting the process allows you to navigate the uncertainties with grace and confidence.

Embracing the Infinite Nature of Love

The Twin Flame connection is a reflection of a greater truth: that love is infinite, boundless, and trans formative. While this journey begins with a connection to another, it ultimately leads you back to yourself and the universal love that flows through all things.

How to Embrace Infinite Love:

- Celebrate the connections in your life that uplift and inspire you.
- Extend kindness and compassion to others, recognizing our shared humanity.
- Reaffirm your own worthiness of love, joy, and fulfillment.

By aligning with the infinite nature of love, you transcend the limitations of fear, doubt, and separation.

The Path Ahead

As this chapter of your journey concludes, a new one begins. Armed with the insights and growth you've achieved, you are ready to move forward with clarity, purpose, and an open heart.

Whether your path leads to reunion, continued self-discovery, or entirely new experiences, trust that each step is meaningful. Embrace the unknown with curiosity and courage, knowing that your soul's evolution is always unfolding in perfect harmony.

Your Sacred Journey

The Twin Flame journey is more than a relationship; it is a sacred opportunity to uncover the truth of who you are and the limitless power of love. By embracing every aspect of this path—the joy, the pain, the lessons, and the growth—you honor not only your connection with your Twin Flame but also the profound beauty of your own soul.

Ultimately when you find the love within it opens you to the opportunity to experience that same love externally through another.

May your journey be one of healing, joy, and transformation, and may the love you discover illuminate every corner of your life.

Epilogue

As we come to the close of this exploration, it is important to remember that the twin flame journey is not an end but an ongoing evolution. It is a path that leads us deeper into the essence of who we are, offering opportunities to grow, to love, and to discover our divine purpose. This journey, while unique to each individual, holds universal lessons about connection, transformation, and the enduring power of love.

Twin flames remind us that love is not merely a feeling—it is a force of nature, capable of transcending time, space, and even our own limitations. They challenge us to see beyond the surface, to embrace our shadow and light, and to step fully into our authentic selves. Through the fire of this connection, we are shaped into more expansive versions of ourselves, open to the infinite possibilities of what love can create.

But perhaps the greatest revelation of the twin flame journey is that the love we seek in another is already within us. Whether or not the earthly union of twin flames comes to pass, the lessons they impart guide us toward self-awareness, self-compassion, and self-acceptance. In this way, every step of the twin flame journey brings us closer to the ultimate truth: that we are already whole, already connected, and already worthy of the love we desire.

As you move forward, may you carry the insights and inspiration of this journey with you. May you find courage in moments of doubt, grace in times of challenge, and joy in the beauty of connection. And above all, may you never lose sight of the sacred truth that the journey itself is the destination.

With love and light,

Kimberley

Afterword

As this book draws to a close, I want to take a moment to reflect on the incredible journey we've shared. Writing about twin flames has been both an exploration of the soul and an act of love—a way to give voice to a connection that defies simple explanation and transcends the boundaries of conventional relationships.

Twin flames are not just about romance or the union of two souls. They are about the larger tapestry of life, the intricate weaving of growth, love, and self-discovery. They challenge us to face our shadows, embrace our truths, and rise to our highest potential. In this way, the twin flame journey is not just a path of connection but a profound spiritual awakening.

Through these pages, I have sought to capture the beauty and complexity of this path—not as an authority, but as a fellow traveler. It is my hope that this book has provided clarity where there was confusion, solace where there was pain, and inspiration where there was doubt. More than anything, I hope it has served as a reminder that you are never alone in this journey. Whether you are united with your twin flame, separated by time and space, or simply discovering yourself, you are part of a vast, interconnected story of love and transformation.

The twin flame journey teaches us that love is infinite, that it exists not only between two people but within ourselves and all around us. As you continue forward, may you carry this truth with you. May you find peace in the knowing that every step—whether smooth or challenging—is a step toward your greater self. And may you always trust in the divine timing of your life, knowing that the universe unfolds as it should.

Thank you for allowing me to be a part of your journey. The love you seek, the love you feel, and the love you are—these are the gifts of the twin flame path. Cherish them, and let them guide you toward the light within.

With heartfelt gratitude,

Kimberley

Resources and Practices for the Twin Flame Journey

The Twin Flame journey can be both profound and challenging, offering opportunities for deep growth, healing, and self-discovery. To navigate this path effectively, many individuals find it helpful to incorporate supportive practices and resources into their lives.

This chapter provides practical tools, recommended readings, and spiritual techniques to assist you on your journey, whether you are exploring the concept of Twin Flames for the first time or seeking deeper alignment with your connection.

1. Spiritual Practices for Self-Awareness and Growth

Developing self-awareness is a cornerstone of the Twin Flame journey. These practices can help you connect with your inner self, process emotions, and find clarity amidst challenges.

Meditation and Mindfulness

- Practice daily meditation to calm the mind, enhance self-awareness, and connect with your higher self.
- Explore guided meditations specifically designed for Twin

Flames, focusing on themes like healing, surrender, and self-love.

Journaling

- Keep a Twin Flame journal to reflect on your thoughts, emotions, and experiences.
- Use prompts like:
- "What lessons am I learning from this connection?"
- "How can I nurture myself during this phase?"

Energy Work

- Engage in energy healing practices such as Reiki, chakra balancing, or sound healing to release blockages and restore harmony.
- Focus on opening the heart chakra to deepen your capacity for unconditional love.

2. Tools for Emotional Healing

Navigating the emotional intensity of the Twin Flame journey requires tools that promote healing and balance.

Emotional Freedom Techniques (EFT)

- Use tapping techniques to release stress, anxiety, or emotional pain.

Visualization Exercises

- Imagine a protective, golden light surrounding you, providing safety and peace during emotionally intense moments.
- Visualize cutting energetic cords when feelings of attachment or overwhelm arise.

Affirmations for Healing

- Repeat positive affirmations daily, such as:
- "I am whole and complete within myself."
- "I release all fear and embrace love."
- "I trust the journey and its divine timing."

3. Building Spiritual Resilience

Spiritual resilience helps you remain grounded and connected to your higher purpose, even during challenging phases of the journey.

Grounding Practices

- Spend time in nature, walking barefoot or meditating under the open sky.
- Incorporate grounding crystals like hematite or black tourmaline into your daily routine.

Rituals for Surrender

- Perform simple rituals to release control and trust the divine plan. For example:
- Write down fears or worries on paper and burn it safely as a symbolic act of surrender.

Connecting with Guides

- Develop a relationship with your spiritual guides through meditation or prayer. Ask for guidance, protection, and clarity regarding your Twin Flame journey.

4. Recommended Books and Resources

Reading about Twin Flames and spiritual growth can provide insights and support. Consider exploring the following titles:

- "The Untethered Soul" by Michael A. Singer: A guide to freeing yourself from limiting beliefs and emotional pain.
- "Journey of Souls" by Dr. Michael Newton: Insights into soul connections and the purpose of reincarnation.
- "You Can Heal Your Life" by Louise Hay: Techniques for self-love, healing, and personal transformation.

5. Connecting with the Twin Flame Community

Finding support from others on similar journeys can be

invaluable. Consider joining:

- **Online Forums:** Participate in discussions on Twin Flame-specific forums or social media groups.
- **Support Groups:** Look for local or virtual support groups focused on spiritual growth and self-discovery.
- **Workshops and Retreats:** Attend events designed to foster connection, healing, and understanding of Twin Flame dynamics.

Engaging with a community can provide encouragement, shared experiences, and a sense of belonging.

6. Daily Practices for Self-Love and Balance

Incorporating daily habits that nurture self-love and balance can help you stay grounded and aligned throughout the Twin Flame journey.

Morning Rituals

- **Begin your day with meditation, gratitude journaling, or affirmations to set a positive tone.**

Mindful Movement

- **Practice yoga, tai chi, or another form of movement that combines physical activity with mindfulness.**

Evening Reflections

- End your day with a gratitude practice, reflecting on the lessons and blessings of the day.

By making these practices part of your routine, you create a strong foundation for navigating the Twin Flame experience with resilience and grace.

7. Embracing Flexibility and Trust

While resources and practices can provide valuable guidance, the Twin Flame journey is ultimately a personal and evolving experience. It's essential to remain flexible and trust your intuition.

Key Reminders:

- Listen to Your Inner Voice: Trust your instincts when deciding which practices or resources resonate with you.
- Be Patient with Yourself: Healing and growth take time; allow yourself to move at your own pace.
- Honor Your Path: Every Twin Flame journey is unique— there is no "right" way to navigate it.

By embracing flexibility and trust, you open yourself to the wisdom and transformation inherent in the journey.

A Toolbox for Transformation

The Twin Flame journey is a sacred path of love, growth, and self-discovery. While the challenges may feel overwhelming at times, the tools and resources available can provide clarity, support, and empowerment.

As you explore the practices outlined in this chapter, remember that the most important resource is your own inner wisdom. Trust yourself, honor your journey, and embrace the trans formative power of this extraordinary connection.

Practices to Cultivate Trust:

- **Affirmation of Surrender:** Repeat affirmations like, "I trust that my journey is guided by divine wisdom."
- **Patience and Presence:** Focus on living fully in the present moment rather than anticipating future outcomes.
- **Signs and Synchronicities:** Pay attention to spiritual signs that reaffirm you are on the right path.

Trusting the divine plan brings peace and clarity, even in moments of uncertainty.

Integrating the Lessons of the Journey

The ultimate purpose of the Twin Flame connection is not only to foster growth within the relationship but also to enrich every aspect of your life. The lessons learned along the way can be integrated into your relationships, work, and personal endeavors.

Steps for Integration:

1. **Reflect on Growth:** Identify key lessons you've learned and how they have transformed your understanding of love and self.
2. **Apply Insights:** Use your newfound wisdom to improve your relationships, decision-making, and overall well-being.
3. **Share Your Journey:** If it feels right, share your experiences with others, offering encouragement and inspiration.

Integration ensures that the growth achieved through the Twin Flame journey continues to shape and empower your future.

Embracing the Infinite Nature of Love

One of the most profound lessons of the Twin Flame journey is the realization that love is infinite and ever-present. While the connection with your Twin Flame is extraordinary, it is also a reflection of the boundless love that exists within and around you.

Ways to Embrace Love's Infinite Nature:

- **Self-Love:** Recognize that the love you seek begins within.
- **Universal Love:** Extend compassion and kindness to all beings, understanding that we are all connected.
- **Gratitude for Connection:** Appreciate the relationships in

your life that bring joy, support, and inspiration.

The journey teaches that love is not limited to one person or outcome but is an expansive force that transforms and uplifts.

Moving Forward with Clarity and Courage

As you continue your Twin Flame journey, remember that every step—whether joyous or challenging—contributes to your growth and evolution. Moving forward requires courage, clarity, and a commitment to your own well-being.

Guiding Principles for Moving Forward:

- **Prioritize Healing:** Continue to nurture your emotional and spiritual health through self-care and reflection.
- **Stay Open:** Embrace the possibilities of life with curiosity and hope, trusting that each experience has meaning.
- **Be True to Yourself:** Align your actions with your values, passions, and inner wisdom.

Moving forward is not about forgetting the past but about carrying its lessons into a brighter and more authentic future.

A Journey Without End

The Twin Flame journey is not defined by its destination but by the transformation it inspires along the way. Each phase, connection, and lesson contributes to the unfolding of your soul's highest potential.

As you walk this path, may you find strength in the challenges,
joy in the discoveries, and love in every step. Your journey
is sacred, unique, and infinitely valuable—an extraordinary
expression of your soul's evolution.

BIBLIOGRAPHY CITING and REFERENCES

1 https://www.masterclass.com/articles/twin-flame

2 https://www.today.com/life/twin-flames-meaning-rcna1 23046Rachel Bernstein, a licensed marriage and family therapist specializing in cult intervention and re-acclimation

Below are warning signs and red flags that a person may be an abuser, according to the National Coalition Against Domestic Violence (NCADV) https://ncadv.org/signs-of-abuse :

ï possessiveness

ï extreme jealousy

ï bad temper

ï cruelty to animals

ï verbal abuse

ï antiquated beliefs about the gender roles in relationships

ï forced sex or disregard for a person's unwillingness to have sex

ï extremely controlling behavior

ï sabotage of partner's birth control methods or refusal to honor agreed-upon methods

ï blaming behavior

ï controls all finances

ï accusations about partner flirting or having an affair

ï controlling how a partner acts and what they wear
ï demeaning the partner privately or publicly
ï embarrassing or humiliating partner in front of others
ï harassing the partner at work
ï hindering the partner from working or going to school

For anonymous, confidential help available 24/7, call the National Domestic Violence Hotline at 1-800-799-7233 (SAFE) or 1-800-787-3224 (TTY) now.

These references can provide further insight and guidance for those seeking to deepen their understanding of Twin Flames and spiritual growth.

Books on Twin Flames and Spiritual Growth

- Hay, Louise. *You Can Heal Your Life*. Hay House Publishing, 1984.
- Newton, Dr. Michael. *Journey of Souls: Case Studies of Life Between Lives*. Llewellyn Publications, 1994.
- Singer, Michael A. *The Untethered Soul: The Journey Beyond Yourself*. New Harbinger Publications, 2007.

Books on Self-Discovery and Emotional Healing

- Brown, Brené. *The Gifts of Imperfection: Let Go of Who You Think You're Supposed to Be and Embrace Who You Are*. Hazelden Publishing, 2010.
- Tolle, Eckhart. *The Power of Now: A Guide to Spiritual Enlightenment*. New World Library, 1997.
- Chopra, Deepak. *The Seven Spiritual Laws of Success*.

Amber-Allen Publishing, 1994.

Online Resources and Communities

- MindBodyGreen: Resources on emotional healing, mindfulness, and spiritual growth.
- Chakra Healing: Guides for balancing energy and fostering emotional resilience.

Scientific and Psychological Perspectives

- Levine, Amir, and Rachel S.F. Heller. *Attached: The New Science of Adult Attachment and How It Can Help You Find—and Keep—Love*. TarcherPerigee, 2010.
- Siegel, Daniel J. *The Mindful Brain: Reflection and Attunement in the Cultivation of Well-Being*. W.W. Norton & Company, 2007.

About the Author

Dr. Taylor is a writer, researcher, and spiritual seeker with a passion for exploring the mysteries of love, connection, and transformation. For over a decade, Dr. Kimberley has delved into the world of twin flames, gathering insights, stories, and wisdom to help others navigate this profound journey. When not writing, Dr. Kimberley can be found teaching, meditating, traveling, or playing with her beloved grandchildren .

You can connect with me on:
🌐 https://www.drkimberleytaylor.com
f https://www.facebook.com/kimberleyhypnoreiki

Subscribe to my newsletter:
✉ https://www.drkimberleytaylor.com